GANGS AND OUTLAWS of
WESTERN PENNSYLVANIA

··

THOMAS WHITE + MICHAEL HASSETT

THE
History
PRESS

For Dr. Edward T. Brett,
mentor and friend

CONTENTS

Acknowledgements   9
Introduction   13

Paul Jaworski and the Flathead Gang   17
The Cooley Gang—Fayette County's Notorious Outlaws   27
Pittsburgh's Earliest Bank Heist   51
The Maug "Mob"   57
A Violent End to a Crime Spree   67
Glenn and Irene—Western Pennsylvania's Bonnie and Clyde   73
Robbery on the Tracks   89
The Biddle Boys Escape   95

Selected Bibliography   113
Index   121
About the Authors   127

ACKNOWLEDGEMENTS

Collecting and researching the stories of these outlaws required the help and support of many people. I want to thank my wife, Justina, and my children, Tommy and Marisa, for allowing me the time to complete this project and for their support. For their continued encouragement, I also want to thank my brother, Ed, and my father, Tom. My mother, Jean, who passed away unexpectedly while I was working on this manuscript, set me on a course of intellectual curiosity at a young age and will always influence any project that I work on. Paul Demilio, Zaina Boulos and Elizabeth Williams all spent time proofreading and editing for me, and their input and suggestions were greatly appreciated. Many other people helped in a variety of ways while we worked on this project. They include Angelle Pryor, Louis Ransom, Gerard O'Neil, Jona Dumbleton, Dr. Joseph Rishel, Dr. Perry Blatz, Dr. Joshua Forrest, Tony Lavorgne, Kurt Wilson, Ken Whiteleather, Brian McKee, Dan Simkins, Brett Cobbey, Brian Hallam, Robert Stakeley, Will and Missy Goodboy and Vince Grubb.

—Thomas

While working on this project, many people provided me with encouragement and support. I want to thank my mom, Joanne, and dad, Thomas, whose love and support give me the courage and confidence to pursue whatever I choose to set my mind to, as well as my siblings, Brandon,

ACKNOWLEDGEMENTS

Erin and Josh, for their continued encouragement and love. I would also like to thank the many aunts, uncles and cousins whose enthusiasm and love have motivated me throughout this project, as well as any other endeavor I undertake. My La Roche College Writers' Center family helped me grow into the writer I am today, especially Cadwell Turnbull, Anju Manandhar, Vanessa Byer, Chris Abbott, Larry Ganni and Therese Joseph, who were there to read and reread my many drafts, offering advice and supporting me through the many ups and downs while writing this book. I would like to especially thank Jessica Ganni, whose continual friendship, motivation and midnight pots of tea were integral to the completion of this project. You all hold a very dear and special place in my heart. I would also like to thank the many educators I have had throughout my life who instilled in me the love of learning and who have helped shape me into the person I am today. To Charles Saunders and Tiffany Lee, whose friendship and encouragement have helped me to grow in ways I never thought possible. Lastly, I would like to thank Thomas White for inviting me on this project and for his continual guidance and patience through the many steps of this book's life.

—Michael

Numerous archivists, librarians and local historians provided us with information and sources as we went about our research. At the New Castle Public Library, Chris Fabian, Katie Minteer, Kelly Norman and Dennis McCullough all assisted Michael as he researched Glenn Dague and Irene Schroeder. Anna Marry Mooney, Dwight Copper and Andrew Henley of the Lawrence County Historical Society also provided vital information and images of the outlaw couple. Chris Lilley, a descendant of the Cooley family, generously shared his large collection of research on the Cooley Gang with us, as did Patricia Forman, who is a descendant of Jacob Prinkey, the gang's most well-known victim. Laura Jaros and Jason Jaros, also descendants of the Cooley family, provided very useful leads. Genealogist and researcher Kathryn Cooley Miller and Vicki Leonelli of the Pennsylvania Department of the Uniontown Public Library helped us track down the photo of the Cooley Gang. Mary Harmon of the Prospect Area Preservation Society and John Schalcosky of the Ross Township Historical Society both supplied us with material on the Biddle Boys. Stephan Bosnyak, who runs an excellent website chronicling the history of Dead Man's Hollow, provided sources detailing the McKeesport Trolley

Robbery. We could not have finished that section without his help. The staff of the Library and Archives at the Heinz History Center was helpful as usual, especially Art Louderback and Matt Strauss. We would also like to thank Hannah Cassilly and the rest of the staff of The History Press for giving us the opportunity to write this book.

INTRODUCTION

When one thinks of armed bandits riding through the countryside, outlaws engaging in shootouts with police, bank heists, train robberies and daring escapes from prison, western Pennsylvania is usually not the first place to come to mind as a setting for such events. Yet all of the aforementioned crimes and the associated chaos did occur here, and sometimes more frequently than one might expect. The interesting and tragic stories of the outlaws who perpetrated these crimes are an often-overlooked part of the region's history. We hope that this book will help to fill in some of those details in the collective story of western Pennsylvania. At the very least, it can serve as a reminder that the violent crimes we unfortunately hear about so often in the news are not a new phenomenon. Every generation has been forced to deal with its own brand of criminals.

One of the first questions we were asked when we set out to write a book about gangs and outlaws in western Pennsylvania was "Are there enough of them to fill a book?" In fact, we were asked that question numerous times as our work progressed. The answer was always "Yes, more than enough." While researching western Pennsylvania's criminal past, we discovered so much material that we were forced to scale back the scope of our original project. Initially, we had intended to include bootleggers and organized crime syndicates, such as the Volpe brothers, John Bazzano Sr., Stefano Monastero and other parts of the Pittsburgh crime family. We had also planned on covering Pittsburgh's Tong Wars and groups such as the Black Hand. As time went on, we realized that "organized" crime could receive its own volume, and if it were included, we would have exceeded the limitations of this book.

Instead, we chose to focus on the more brazen outlaws and gangs that tended to commit violent and sometimes public robberies (in the style of John Dillinger). These were the kinds of outlaws that led local historian C. Wallace Abel to label the area the "Wild, Wild East." Even with a narrower focus, we could not, by any means, include every outlaw or gang of outlaws that operated in western Pennsylvania. Still, our selection process remained simple. We picked the ones that we found most interesting and the ones on which we could find the most information. If we did not discuss your "favorite" local gang or outlaw, we apologize in advance. We think, however, that we have assembled a collection of intriguing tales. Among these pages you will find the story of the ruthless Flathead Gang, which pulled off the world's first armored car robbery in Bethel Park and whose leader managed to escape from the Allegheny County Jail. We also recount the story of the Cooley Gang, a band of Fayette County thieves who held the locals in fear and were compared to infamous western outlaws. You will be introduced to the perpetrators of Pittsburgh's first major bank robbery, learn the details of a crime spree that ended with a violent confrontation near Ellwood City and discover two of the region's biggest train robberies that occurred in Erie and Cambria Counties. Another chapter covers the lives of western Pennsylvania's outlaw couple Glenn Dague and Irene Schroeder, who committed a series of robberies and shot a police officer. You will meet the Maug Gang, which made a habit of robbing trolley car barns and later escaped from Western Penitentiary. And of course, no survey of western Pennsylvania criminals would be complete without an account of the Biddle Boys, who escaped from prison with the help of the warden's wife.

Reconstructing the criminal careers of these outlaws was a tedious process, especially the further back in time that we went. Often there was very little information available. Another problem that we encountered was that we found contradictory accounts of many of the crimes. This is a common occurrence with newspapers since they gather more facts as time passes and later update their stories, but occasionally the contradictory accounts came from law enforcement officials themselves. That being said, we have done our best to compile the most historically accurate accounts of these gangs and outlaws as possible. We hope you enjoy this trip into the dark side of western Pennsylvania's history.

PAUL JAWORSKI AND THE FLATHEAD GANG

It was almost noon on March 11, 1927, when an armored car belonging to the Brinks Company turned on to what is today Brightwood Road in the quiet Pittsburgh suburb of Bethel Park. It was Friday, and the car was carrying the payroll for the employees of the nearby Coverdale mine, which was owned by the Pittsburgh Terminal Coal Company. Four armed guards rode in the armored vehicle, while two more guards followed in a trail car. As far as the men knew, it was just another routine cash delivery. They had no idea they were about to become the victims of the first ever armored car robbery.

Just off to the side of the road lurked members of the Flathead Gang and its leader, Paul Jaworski (sometimes spelled Jawarski). The gang members had been committing violent robberies in both Pittsburgh and Detroit for several years, and they were about to attempt their biggest score to date. Using large amounts of black powder, Jaworski constructed two homemade land mines that the gang hid under loose patches of pavement on the road. The mines were connected by wire to a box and plunger hidden in the nearby bushes. It is not known how the outlaws learned of the armored car's route, but they were well prepared for its arrival. Nine members of the gang were hidden nearby and were ready to shoot if necessary.

As the armored car drove past the gang, Jaworski pushed down the plunger. The resulting explosion sent the vehicle tumbling. It came to rest on its roof. Inside, the upside-down guards were either dazed or unconscious. The trail car, which also felt the impact of the explosion, crashed into the depression that the explosion left in the road. Both of the car's occupants were alive but were reeling from the shock. The Flathead Gang wasted no time in securing the armored car's cargo. Damage to the vehicle's wooden floor and frame allowed them to access the $104,000 that was in the back (after this robbery, all Brinks cars were given steel floors and frames). The robbers quickly split the loot and fled from the scene toward Washington County in two different cars that had been waiting nearby.

Police launched a search for the bandits immediately. They suspected that the group was still hiding out somewhere in Washington County. After searching for more than twelve hours, the police received a tip from a farmer outside Bentleyville. The man had seen a carload of suspicious men drive up to a nearby farmhouse owned by Joseph Weckoski. Officers and detectives were dispatched to check the premises. When they arrived, they entered the house with guns drawn. After a quick search of the vacant first floor, they crept up the stairs to find a rather nondescript man in the second-floor bedroom who identified himself as Paul Palmer. Officers dragged him downstairs but assumed that he was not a member of the gang. One even described him as a "dumb hunky," but they took him into custody anyway. Three days later, Joseph Weckoski was picked up by police in Detroit. He had fled with the rest of the gang. When he was returned to Pittsburgh, the police learned that Paul Palmer was also wanted in Detroit. After his arrest, Weckoski cracked and told the police everything he knew. For five years he had allowed the Flathead Gang to use his farm as a hideout. He had received $3,000 of the latest heist for harboring the gang. More importantly, he confirmed that the unassuming "Paul Palmer" was actually Paul Jaworski, leader of the Flathead Gang.

Paul Jaworski had not intended to embark on a life of crime. Contrary to what most people believed (and still believe), Jaworski was not ethnically Polish. His real name was Paul Paluszynski, and his family came from Ukraine when he was a child. Paul had been born around 1900, but even he did not know his exact age and date of birth. His family first settled in Braddock, Pennsylvania, before moving to Butler. The family later relocated to Youngstown, Ohio, for a short time only to return to Butler. Jaworski's father finally took the family to Detroit, where they put down more permanent roots. Jaworski felt at home in both western Pennsylvania and the Detroit area and would eventually commit major crimes in both regions. As a boy, Jaworski had wanted to be a farmer, though he worked factory jobs as a young adult. He also considered being a pilot or airplane mechanic but did not have the skills to succeed in aeronautics. In Detroit,

Paul Jaworski and the Flathead Gang

Paul remained restless and directionless, and he started to get into trouble. After being arrested for a few minor offenses, he had an argument with his father over the bad reputation that he was bringing to the family name. As a result, he began to use the last name of Jaworski. Later in his life, when he was on the way to his execution, Jaworski told newspaper reporter Ray Sprigle that he had picked that name because "it's Polish and I hate a damn Pollack anyway. Let them have the disgrace."

Around 1920, Jaworski and some of his accomplices began committing robberies in the Pittsburgh area. It is not known what finally drove Jaworski to launch into a series of violent armed robberies, but once he chose that path, he never went back. Throughout most of the 1920s, the Flathead Gang would travel back and forth between Pittsburgh and Detroit, looking for more lucrative "jobs." The targets were frequently company payrolls, often those of mines, since they were usually large sums. Jaworski led the Flathead Gang when they committed their first well-known holdup in the Pittsburgh suburb of Mount Lebanon in 1922.

At 9:30 a.m. on December 23, a car carrying a Christmas payroll and three company officials left Mount Lebanon heading in the direction of the Beadling mine (along Beadling Road). It was being accompanied by guard Ross Dennis, who was riding just ahead on his motorcycle. They did not go far when a shotgun blast rang out from the side of the road. Dennis was knocked off his motorcycle and severely wounded. The payroll car stopped when he fell, and the three men inside soon heard men yelling outside the vehicle. Six armed figures surrounded the car with guns leveled at the men. The bandits demanded that they put their hands in the air. Just then, Jaworski noticed that Ross Dennis was trying to pull his pistol from his holster as he lay on the ground. The bandit coldly walked up to Dennis, jammed the muzzle of his shotgun against his back and squeezed the trigger. The other members of the gang ordered the three mine officials out of the car and onto the ground. A bag full of money that contained over $20,000 meant for the mine workers was taken from the back seat. As their escape car pulled up, members of the gang damaged both the motorcycle and payroll car so that they could not be pursued. They crowded into their vehicle and headed back to Weckoski's farm.

The gang continued to commit small robberies in the area after the Beadling heist. Many minor crimes that occurred during these years were later attributed to the gang but never proven. Jaworski was not even one of the initial suspects in the Beadling robbery. At one point in 1924, he was wounded by a bar owner during a botched robbery in Pittsburgh.

A postcard depicting the Allegheny County Courthouse in the early twentieth century. *Courtesy of the Library and Archives Division, Senator John Heinz Pittsburgh Regional History Center.*

He was arrested and held in police custody while he recovered from the wound. When he was better, a friend posted the $5,000 bail, and Jaworski disappeared again. He resurfaced in Detroit, where the gang robbed a bank, killing a guard in the process. The Flatheads even committed robberies in Ohio, but all the while they remained essentially invisible to police, who often pinned their crimes on other gangs.

On Christmas Eve 1925, the members of the Flathead Gang decided to help themselves to another Christmas payroll. This time their target was the Mollenauer mine, south of Pittsburgh in Bethel Park. Members of the gang drove up behind payroll guard Isaiah Gump as he was exiting his vehicle at the mine with the satchel of money. As Gump became aware of the men's presence, he reached for his gun. A shot rang out from the outlaws' car, knocking the guard to the ground. Jaworski and another man, possibly longtime gang member Stanley Bodziakowski, ran up to Gump and fired two more shots into him. They took the satchel containing $48,000, got back in their car and fled.

After the murder and robbery, authorities finally seemed to take note of the Flathead Gang. They could not catch them, however, until they received the tip from the farmer in Washington County after the armored car robbery well over a year later. After Jaworski was captured, he took police to an old can buried under a manure pile on the farm. Inside was $36,000 of the stolen armored car money. The rest of the money had been divided up among the members of the Flathead Gang or hidden elsewhere. Jaworski's cooperation did not gain him leniency, nor did he expect it to. He was quickly tried and convicted for the armored car robbery and received a thirty- to sixty-year sentence. Only days later, he was tried again for the murder of Isaiah Gump. He was again convicted but this time sentenced to die in the electric chair. Jaworski had repeatedly stated that he preferred death to a long prison sentence. He just wanted to "get it over with." Paul Jaworski did not realize that his life of crime was not over yet.

On the afternoon of August 18, 1927, Jaworski received a visitor at the Allegheny County Jail. His brother Sam, who also used the last name Jaworski, frequently came to see his imprisoned sibling. There was no indication that this visit would be any different than previous ones. The two men sat and talked for a few minutes in his cell. When they were finished, Sam rose and walked to the door. As the guard prepared to let him out, Sam suddenly drew two .45-caliber pistols. He jammed one into the gut of the guard, demanding that he hold the door open. As Sam and Paul stepped out of the cell, the brother pulled out two more .45s and gave them to Paul. Quickly, guards raced to the scene of the disturbance, but Paul Jaworski opened fire down the hallway. His barrage wounded two and forced others to take cover. At the same time, Sam forced one of the guards to open the next set of locked doors that led into one of the offices by threatening to kill another guard. As the pair made their way out, they passed another block of cells. Paul fired a shot at another prisoner whom he did not like, but the bullet missed. For unknown reasons, Paul paused to release another death row inmate, Jack Vasabinder. Vasabinder was a known drug addict and had the reputation of a crazed killer. He was on death row for shooting and killing a random pedestrian who had refused to give him a quarter. Sam continued to use guards as hostages until the front door of the jail had been opened. A car carrying other members of the Flathead Gang had pulled up to the curb. Paul, Sam and Jack Vasabinder ran down the front steps and got

The "Bridge of Sighs" connecting the Allegheny County Courthouse and Jail, circa 1920. *Authors' collection.*

in after pausing to fire another volley of shots back into the jail. The car sped off before police could intercept it. Despite a thorough manhunt, there was no sign of the Jaworskis or Vasabinder.

Local authorities had little success tracking the gang in the days after the escape because its members had fled the area immediately. Descriptions of the escapees were distributed to all the law enforcement agencies in the Midwest and Northeast. By October, police in Detroit had managed to locate and arrest Sam Jaworski. He was returned to the Allegheny County Jail on October 21 to await trial. He was later convicted and served twelve years in prison. The following month, Pittsburgh police chief J.W. Geisler received a tip from authorities in Montreal that Flathead Gang member Stanley Bodziakowski had been spotted there. The chief and two detectives traveled to Canada and were able to apprehend the outlaw on November 26 and return him to Pittsburgh to stand trial. Though they were successful in apprehending two members of the gang, there was still no sign of the ruthless Paul Jaworski.

Throughout the first half of 1928, Paul remained in Detroit rebuilding his gang and scouting new targets. On June 6, he emerged from hiding to strike again. At 11:00 a.m., Jaworski and four other men casually walked into the offices of the *Detroit News*. All five carried brown paper bags that concealed handguns. The gang quickly made its way to the second floor, where the week's payroll was being processed. They entered the main room and drew their guns. As Jaworski held the workers at bay, members of the gang took all the pay envelopes that were readily available. Just as the gang was exiting, the paymaster emerged from his office and fired a shot toward the door. He was too late. While the gang was coming back down the steps, Detroit police sergeant George Barstad was entering the building. Barstad had been outside and heard the gunshot. Unfortunately for the officer, he walked right into Jaworski at the bottom of the stairwell. The emotionless outlaw and another member of the gang fired quickly, inflicting fatal wounds on Barstad. The gang walked out to the sidewalk where their getaway car waited. The Flathead Gang escaped again, but this time their score was not as big as Jaworski had hoped. He had expected to get $65,000. Instead, the envelopes that the gang had stolen held less than $15,000.

After the *Detroit News* robbery, Jaworski relocated the Flathead Gang to Cleveland. For several months, the outlaws amassed firearms, including machine guns. They were coming up with a daring plan—the Flathead Gang was going to storm the Allegheny County Jail and free Sam Jaworski. But before the plan could be put into motion, fate intervened. On September 13, only days before they were to leave for Pittsburgh, Jaworski and two of his allies were eating at a restaurant on Fleet Avenue. Only a few tables away sat a man from Pittsburgh who had known Paul Jaworski when he was much younger. The man quietly got up and left his table. He walked to a nearby payphone and called the Cleveland Police. Within minutes, police cars screeched to a stop in front of the restaurant. Five policemen got out with their weapons drawn. Jaworski was near the doorway and drew his guns, while his accomplices ran. Thirty-three-year-old Patrolman Anthony Wieczorek was entering the business when the outlaw opened fire. The shots killed Wieczorek where he was standing, and Jaworski kept firing. Another of his bullets ripped through the chest and lung of Patrolman George Effinger. Though Effinger did not die of his wounds immediately, long-term complications claimed his life four years later. Jaworski brazenly charged out the door across Fleet Avenue, keeping the other police pinned with his gunfire. Twenty-seven-year-old Benjamin Majstrek happened to be walking up the street when Jaworski ran into his path. For no reason, the outlaw aimed his pistol and shot Majstrek in the groin.

This photo of Paul Jaworski was taken shortly after his final arrest in Cleveland in 1928. *Authors' collection.*

Paul Jaworski and the Flathead Gang

The outlaw kept going, cutting through a lumberyard and then into a private house on Chambers Avenue. He batted a woman and her child out of the way, ran up the stairs and leapt out of the second-story window only to find his way blocked by a confused and curious crowd. Jaworski turned and went back inside, locking himself in the kitchen. Within moments, the residence was surrounded by dozens of armed policemen. The police ordered him to come out and surrender. Jaworski yelled back, telling them to "come in and get me." The officers responded by throwing tear gas grenades into the house. Determined to die on his feet but unable to see, Jaworski charged onto the porch with a gun in his hand. His eyes were watering heavily from the gas, and he could not aim. Taking advantage of his hesitation, Patrolman Yaro Koudela, who was crouched near the edge of the porch, fired one round from his shotgun. The blast knocked Jaworski off his feet, putting four holes in him. The other officers surrounded and disarmed him as he lay bleeding on the porch. Jaworski was still alive for the moment, but his time as an outlaw had come to an end.

For the next several months, Jaworski was kept under armed guard at a Cleveland hospital while surgeons repaired his wounds. His left leg was partially paralyzed by one of the slugs. Authorities in Cleveland charged him with the murder of Patrolman Wieczorek but agreed to send him back to Pennsylvania since he was already sentenced to death there. They were sure he had killed at least seven people during his stint of robberies. Jaworski himself claimed to have murdered as many as twenty-six people. After being returned to Allegheny County, the state set a date for his execution— December 31, 1928. Jaworski asked for temporary reprieve for the courts to test his sanity, and he was given twenty additional days. He was judged sane and taken to Rockview Penitentiary for execution in mid-January 1929. Journalist Ray Sprigle accompanied the killer on his long final drive from Allegheny County to his place of execution in central Pennsylvania. Throughout the drive, Jaworski revealed details about his crimes and his early life, all the while attempting to appear cool and emotionless. Sprigle noted, however, that he nervously chain smoked stogies up until his time of execution. On the morning of January 21, Paul Jaworski was strapped into the electric chair. His smug arrogance had disappeared, and witnesses described him as being in a daze. An avowed atheist, Jaworski refused the consolation of a priest or minister. The switch was thrown at 7:02 a.m., and the ruthless outlaw who had shown so little respect for the lives of others was declared dead four minutes later.

THE COOLEY GANG

Fayette County's Notorious Outlaws

S amuel Humbert's neighbors in Fairchance, Fayette County, knew that he was a wealthy man, even though he took great care to hide that fact. Born into poverty, Humbert had worked hard in his youth and saved his money. As he aged, he became something of an eccentric and a miser. Though he feigned poverty, he hoarded his wealth, exchanging paper money for gold and silver whenever possible. Townspeople said that he hid his gold and silver in a box somewhere in his home. By the late 1880s, his wife was dead, and he was living alone in a row house just off Main Street. Unfortunately for the old man, his reputation made him a target.

On June 9, 1888, Humbert's life would be dramatically changed. It was around midnight on that early summer evening when Humbert heard the knock at his door. He was, of course, highly suspicious given the late hour and did not initially open it. Instead, he yelled out and asked who was there and what they wanted. On the other side, he heard a man ask if he could have a drink of water. The man's tone must have seemed sincere enough because Humbert left momentarily to retrieve a drink for him. When he returned, he carefully opened the door, only to find two men wearing masks. To his horror, the men lunged forward and forced their way inside. The robbers easily subdued the old man and quickly searched the house. When they found nothing of value, the pair demanded that the old man reveal the location of his gold. Humbert insisted, as he had always done, that he had no money and no possessions of any value. The robbers believed otherwise and quickly lost patience.

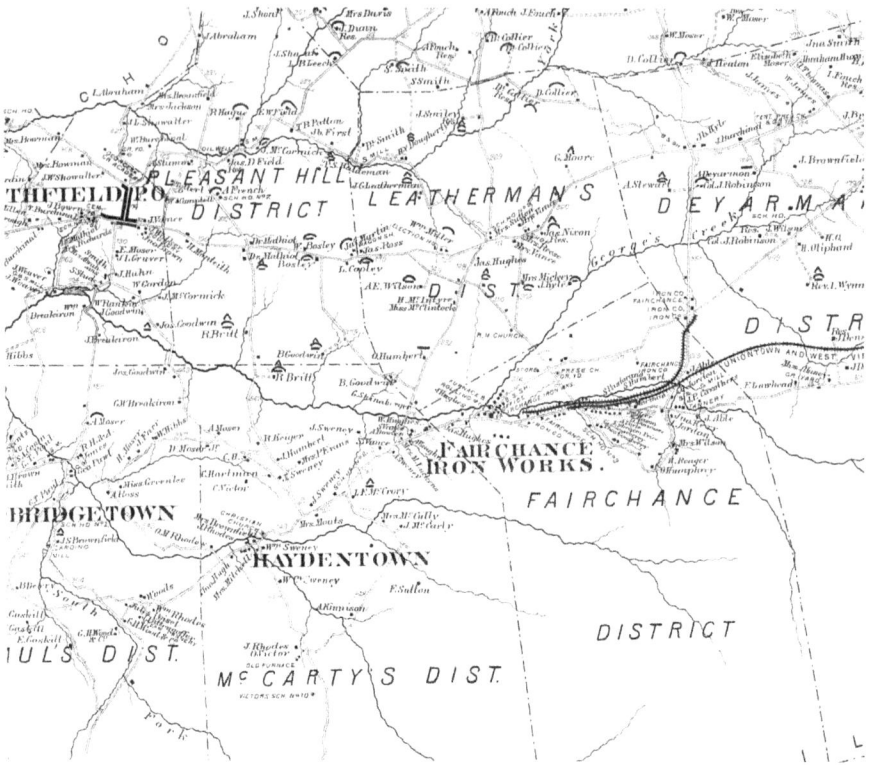

A map of the Fairchance area in Fayette County from an 1872 atlas. *Courtesy of the Library and Archives Division, Senator John Heinz Pittsburgh Regional History Center.*

One of the men lit a candle while the other restrained Humbert. They mercilessly held the flame to his feet in an attempt to force the old man to reveal the hiding place. Despite the pain, Humbert continued to insist that there was nothing valuable to be found in the house. The robbers became increasingly frustrated. They dragged Humbert across the room and began to hold his feet over the hearth. Humbert writhed in pain as his feet burned and blistered. Finally, to avoid further agony, he blurted out some clue as to where the box of gold and silver might be found. The two invaders tore the interior of his house to pieces looking for it. They knocked items off the walls, ripped up carpets and floorboards and knocked over furniture. Still, they found nothing. When it became clear that they would not get anything from the old man, they bound his hands and feet and left him on the floor. The robbers slipped away into the darkness. Samuel Humbert did not know it at the time, but he had become the first "official" victim of the Cooley Gang.

The Cooley Gang

When Humbert told his neighbors and the authorities about the invasion of his home, not everyone believed him. He was viewed as an odd man, and some thought it was another attempt to appear impoverished. Humbert's wounds were very real, however, and after the attack, he suffered heart problems. His health deteriorated, and he died the following year. (On his deathbed, he attempted to tell a friend the location of his gold but suffered a coughing fit and died in mid-sentence.) It would not be long, though, until most residents of Fayette County came to believe the story of his attack. The Cooley Gang had begun a reign of terror that would last for more than four years.

The outlaws, who fashioned themselves equals to the infamous James Gang, committed a long string of robberies and dramatic home invasions between 1888 and 1892 that made them the scourge of the region. Though they would be accused of many crimes and robberies that they did not commit, the gang's members would be implicated or convicted in many others. The leaders of the gang were Frank Cooley and his younger brother Andrew Jackson Cooley, better known as Jack. Both men grew up on their father's property near Fairchance. Frank and Jack were two of the eleven boys and five girls born to Lucius "Lute" Cooley. Many of the other brothers eventually ran with the gang for various periods of time.

Though the Cooley Gang only gained widespread notoriety in 1888 after the Humbert robbery, its members' criminal careers actually began much earlier. On May 20, 1881, at the age of seventeen, Frank was kicked out of the house after repeatedly causing problems. He wandered the Chestnut Ridge, committing petty thefts and stealing chickens. At some point, he was joined by his brothers Dick and Jack and his old friend Jack Ramsey. Ramsey, who was a resident of McClellandtown, later became a key member of the group. He was thought to be the gang's mastermind, selecting wealthy and isolated individuals whom they could rob. The Cooleys got in trouble right from the start. By the end of 1881, Jack had been arrested for theft and taken to Uniontown. After only a few days in jail, he somehow managed to escape and fled back into the mountains. Not long after, Lute Cooley had a change of heart and welcomed his boys back for visits. It was reported by neighbors that he seemed to be coming to terms with the lifestyle they had decided to lead. The Cooley boys continued bullying certain neighbors and committing minor crimes, but they did not draw much attention until 1884, when Frank and Dick were arrested for assault and battery and held for trial in Uniontown. Both were found guilty and ordered to pay fines of twenty-five dollars plus court costs. The brothers refused, and both served time in jail instead. Shortly after, another Cooley brother named William appeared in court, charged with assaulting Sallie Hibbs. The case was eventually settled out of court but seemingly led William and Oliver Cooley to follow in Frank and Jack's footsteps.

Despite the legal trouble, the Cooleys and their associates did little to alter their usual pattern of stealing from and intimidating local farmers. Two years later, in March 1886, Frank and Dick were in trouble again. Both were charged with assaulting a farmer named James Bowell. The Cooleys stayed in the mountains, however, out of the reach of law enforcement. Not a month went by before William and Jack were also charged with assaulting a man named John Rhodes and a woman named Mintie McCullough. As in the case of their brothers, neither man was apprehended. The would-be gang was becoming more aggressive and seemed to be developing a sense of being untouchable. This feeling was cemented when more charges were leveled against Dick Cooley in December 1886. This time, they were breaking and entering and receiving stolen property. Authorities pursued Dick Cooley for two weeks before abandoning the hunt. Frank and the gang may have believed they had the upper hand, but the authorities did not want to invest too much time and money chasing what they perceived as a group of small-time thieves and muggers. Their opinions would soon change with the gang's modus operandi.

Frank and his fledgling band of robbers learned the ruthless techniques of torture that they would become known for using in the mid-1880s from the Lewis Gang, also known as the McClellandtown Gang. Charles Lewis, the head of the gang, was repeatedly described as sadistic and had practiced a similar style of home invasion and robbery. Lewis frequently tormented his victims with fire. After a string of violent robberies throughout Fayette and Somerset Counties, the Lewis Gang was apprehended by a posse and arrested. Jack Ramsey seemed to have some connection with the Lewis Gang but had already gone his own way by the time of Lewis's capture. Soon, the Cooley Gang made its presence known throughout the countryside in an equally dramatic fashion.

Frank Cooley added more members to his gang as the decade progressed. The other main members of the group were Brent Frye, Sam Yeager, Charlie David, Jim Hutchinson, William Martin, William Turner and the "Queen," Lyda Pastorious (also known as Lida Patterson). Though the beautiful Pastorious, who was Frank's lover, did not usually participate in the crimes directly, she often accompanied the Cooley Gang and had no qualms about helping them spend their loot. She allegedly also played an integral part in planning the gang's activities with Ramsey. Occasionally, other men would assist the gang on its raids, but they were not part of the original inner circle. Most of the members were reportedly under the age of thirty. The gang was successful, in part, because it intimidated the residents of southern Fayette County into not revealing its whereabouts when the authorities came looking for the gang. The lack of assistance from the local community made law enforcement officials hesitant to try to arrest the gang at the Cooley homestead or in public places. When the members of the gang were being pursued they used a variety of hiding places, including Delany's Cave (now Laurel Caverns). The gang may also have been receiving warnings from sympathetic (or frightened) local officials.

The Humbert robbery marked the beginning of a new era for the gang. Even though its first attempt was ultimately unsuccessful, home invasion and torture had worked for the Lewis Gang. It also attracted attention in the local press, which in turn enhanced the menacing reputation of the group. After laying low for close to half a year, Frank decided that it was time to strike again. In December 1888, the Cooley Gang selected a new target: a sixty-year-old spinster named Mollie Ross. Ross lived alone on a farm almost four miles outside of Fairchance. As in the case with Samuel Humbert, rumors circulated in the community that Ross had a substantial amount of wealth. Papers later reported that Frank Cooley had been told that several thousand dollars were hidden on Ross's property. Late in the evening on December 10, Frank and two members of the gang loaded their Smith and Wesson pistols and Marlin repeating rifles, put on their masks and set out for the Ross homestead.

Just after midnight, the gang came to Ross's front door and found it locked. The Cooleys decided to smash a nearby window to gain access to the house. One can imagine the terror Mollie Ross felt as she heard the window shatter. She was in her bed, as she had been all evening, suffering from a debilitating attack of rheumatism. She could not even get up to run away. Frank Cooley walked into her room and right up to her bed. In a menacing tone, he demanded to know where she kept her money. Even though she was terrified, Ross refused to tell the men where the money was. Frank then threatened to kill her if she did not reveal the hiding place, but Ross defiantly stated that they would never get her money.

The gang was finished playing games. They dragged the woman out of bed and tied her to a chair. Frank then told Jack Ramsey to "bare her feet and hand me a candle." With a cold stare, Frank brought the flame to the bottom of Ross's foot. He cruelly held the candle in place for almost two

The Cooley Gang, circa 1890. *Left to right*: Brent Frye, Sam Yeager, Frank Cooley, Jack Ramsey and Jack Cooley. *Courtesy of the Uniontown Public Library, Pennsylvania Department.*

minutes. Cooley gave the woman another opportunity to reveal the location of the money, but she flatly refused. The candle was held to her feet three more times, but Ross refused to give in. Finally, Frank became so angry that he clenched his fist and punched Mollie Ross in the face. As in the case with Humbert, the gang decided to tear the house to pieces hoping to find the stash. Accounts vary as to what they did find. Initial reports indicated that they found no more than $5, and some said as little as twelve cents. At least one account from a few years later stated that the gang discovered $600 in bank notes during the ransacking of the house. When they were finished searching, they untied Mollie Ross but warned her not to go for help. Cooley promised to return and kill her if she did. Ross waited until the next morning before going to her neighbors.

All of Fayette County was shocked by the brutality of the crime, especially since it was perpetrated against a sickly woman. Though they wore masks, the gang did little to hide its members' identities. The Cooley Gang was now being considered a serious threat, and the call went out for the arrests of its members. Warrants were issued for Frank and his accomplices within days. Many residents in the southern part of the county were afraid of the retaliation that they would face if they turned the gang in to the authorities but were hoping that local law enforcement would somehow be able to handle the outlaws.

The local officials were able to catch up with Frank and arrest him. The rest of the gang remained free, however. On December 27, 1888, Frank was released from jail after Lute Cooley and Lyda Pastorious posted $1,000 in bail. However, after a brief trial on June 9, 1889, he was convicted and returned to the Uniontown jail to await sentencing. He would not be staying. In December, Frank still had not received his sentence, though that fact was soon irrelevant. Frank and three other inmates decided that it was time to leave. At some point in the previous days, a visitor or guard had slipped the men case knives, which they modified into primitive saws. Like in the plot of an old movie, the men relentlessly sawed away at their cell bars late at night when the guards were not watching. When the bars were cut, Cooley and an accomplice slipped out into the main hallway. Using pieces of a gas burner as a tool, the men removed the bolts from the door of the main office. The pair quickly retrieved the cell keys from the desk and released the other two prisoners. Two young black men, who had been arrested the previous evening for a minor altercation, refused to leave. (They later provided the police with the details of the escape.) Frank and the others then bolted out into the darkness and scattered. The escape only added to his reputation and his growing ego.

After a few months, the Cooley Gang apparently resumed its practice of harassing and robbing the people of Fayette County. Muggings, livestock thefts and other crimes were committed on a regular basis. Many of the victims were too intimidated to report the crimes to the authorities, and more than one resident believed that local law enforcement was also too frightened to apprehend the gang. Some of the crimes were likely committed by other thieves trying to capitalize on the gang's reputation. Still, until the summer of 1891, the exploits of the gang were not widely known outside of Fayette County. That changed in June of that year, when the newspapers in Pittsburgh and other regions began to cover the gang's activities with great interest. Soon there were several stories a month that discussed, often in a highly dramatized fashion, the current crimes of the Cooley boys. One headline from June in the *Pittsburg Dispatch* read "Terrorized by Bandits: Townships in Fayette County Ruled by Robbers." The article described the Cooley Gang's reign of terror over Georges Township. According to the article, it had become so bad that even the women had resorted to carrying firearms to defend themselves, and no one would travel at night. It went on to mention two of the gang's recent despicable acts. First, the gang robbed the Presbyterian church at Haydentown, taking its brand-new carpet. Later that week, the Cooleys paid a visit to one of their critics who lived in Smithfield named Charles Ewing. They burned his house to the ground. Another account from the *New York Times* reported that five masked men, thought to be members of the Cooley Gang, forced their way into William Foster's farmhouse in Franklin Township. At gunpoint, Foster and his housekeeper were bound and gagged. The masked men demanded that he turn over his savings, which amounted to $1,500, and then disappeared into the darkness.

The fearsome portrayal of the gang in the press, whether deserved or not, only emboldened its members. An article from August 3 reported that Frank and Jack walked into a public dance in Fairchance with their Winchester rifles. They mingled with those in attendance after they turned the guns over to a boy who stood nearby at all times in case of trouble. After staying a while, the Cooleys casually took their rifles and disappeared into the nearby woods. Though their presence caused quite a commotion, no one attempted to arrest or detain them. According to Sheriff George McCormick, the gang still had plenty of friends in Fairchance who could have helped facilitate an escape if necessary. Law enforcement officials may have been aware of their activities, but attempting to arrest them there would most likely have been a futile endeavor. As in most cases, friends and family members would

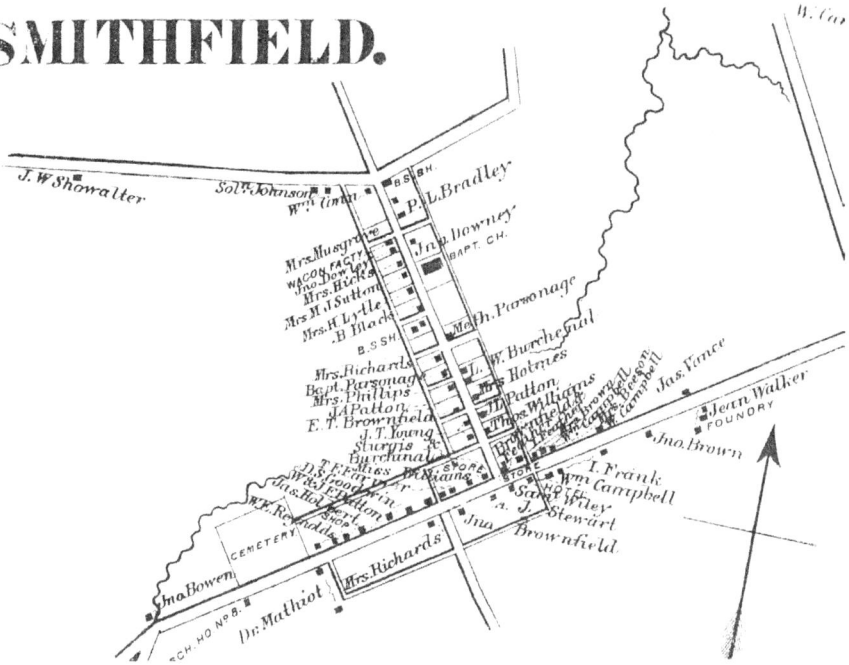

A map of Smithfield in Fayette County from an 1872 atlas. *Courtesy of the Library and Archives Division, Senator John Heinz Pittsburgh Regional History Center.*

regularly warn the Cooleys if the sheriff and his men were anywhere close to them. Still, the ease with which the gang moved about and its brazen public appearances drew more scrutiny from the press, especially from outside Fayette County. Deputy sheriff Joseph Allebaugh told one reporter in November that they would be able to bring the Cooleys to justice if they could offer a sizable reward. Allebaugh believed that Frank Cooley was inherently a coward, but he believed that Jack Ramsey was a coldblooded killer. He ended his statement by saying (in reference to Ramsey), "I know him well, and, so far as he is concerned, I want to keep away from the gang as far as possible." His words did not inspire confidence in the citizens of Fayette County.

More crimes were attributed to the outlaws in November. In front of a schoolyard full of almost one hundred children, Frank and his friends mercilessly beat a peddler named Joel Rosenstein, taking the $51 that he was carrying. After the attack, Rosenstein tried to crawl to a nearby house. When the gang members saw this, they ran back and beat him into unconsciousness.

Cooley and his friends walked away, and no one attempted to stop them. Some of the children ran to get help for the severely injured peddler. On November 19, the *Pittsburg Dispatch* reported that detectives from Pittsburgh had been sent to Fayette County to help with the hunt for the gang. The same article recounted the gang's robbery of the Fairchance Furnace Company. Two members (one most likely being Frank) stormed into the main office on payday and demanded all the cash. The pair made off with $5,000 and disappeared back into the mountains.

On December 20, 1891, the *Pittsburg Dispatch* ran an article that was even more dramatic than the previous ones. The headline compared the Cooley Gang directly to the James Gang, which was by that point the very symbol of western outlaws. It read, "Beats Jesse James. Western Brigandage in Its Palmiest Days Utterly Outdone by the Notorious Cooley Gang." The article first reiterated the state of terror that the people of Fayette County were living under because of the gang. It went on to list a series of recent robberies committed by the group, including the theft of three recently slaughtered pigs from a smokehouse owned by James McCormick, ten barrels of apples from a nearby orchard and ten to fifteen barrels of corn from another farm. Finally, the article detailed an extensive statement from an anonymous Georges Township farmer who had been visiting Pittsburgh the previous day. He told the paper that the gang had twenty-five members, one of whom he had spoken to just days before. The unidentified gang member told the man that the gang was busy scouting for possible victims just over the border in Preston County, West Virginia. He also related that a detective from Pittsburgh attempted to go undercover to gain information on the outlaws. The detective pretended to be a poor and hungry traveler, and he stopped by Jack Cooley's cabin to ask for something to eat. Jack, apparently feeling sorry for the man, invited him in and gave him a good meal. When Frank Cooley arrived later that evening, he spotted the charade and threw the detective out, warning him that if he ever returned he would "put daylight through him quicker than greased lightning." The anonymous farmer went on to say that if the gang believed that you would be friendly toward them, the most they would do is occasionally steal some chickens or food. If you were determined to be hostile to the gang, they "will poison your stock, kill your dogs, and get revenge any way they can."

The Cooleys were now a major news story, and rumors and facts began to swirl together as regional papers raced to gather new reports of the gang's activities. A rumor briefly circulated in the end of December that Frank Cooley had been shot and killed by one of his own friends during a dispute.

The report was false, but it kept the gang in the news. In fact, as that story hit the press, Frank was alive and well and leading his gang into West Virginia, just as predicted by the anonymous farmer. Frank, Jack and two other members of the gang donned masks and robbed the home of Isaac Blaney in Monongalia County. Blaney, his wife and his grandson were held at gunpoint while the gang tore his house apart. The gang left with $200 and apparently crossed back into Pennsylvania. During another raid in Preston County, Frank Cooley, Sam Yeager and Rufus Meyers robbed the home of a man named Yost. Their rough treatment of the old man resulted in his death. Authorities in West Virginia were outraged, and both Preston County and Monongalia County offered to contribute to the reward for Frank and the gang.

Ironically, the day after the story of the West Virginia robbery ran in the papers, an attorney from Uniontown claimed that there was no Cooley Gang. Frank Fuller stated that many of the tales told about the gang were false, citing the report of Frank's death, and that the family just had a bad reputation. He described them as "rough characters who trade horses and get along doing as little work as possible, but do not have a gang as reported." Fuller owned a farm in southern Fayette County that was never targeted by the gang. Strangely enough, a few days later on January 2, 1892, two Pittsburghers also defended the gang after a visit to Fayette County. George Meyers and George Mashey spent a day at the Cooley homestead. They described the Cooleys as tough, uneducated mountaineers but emphasized that they were harmless and of no danger. Meyers and Mashey doubted that the men had the courage to commit a robbery or invade a house and stated that their neighbors seemed to get along with them well.

Apparently, the Cooleys were not as simple as their visitors would have them appear. They clearly understood the value of some favorable publicity. Though Frank and the others might have relished the comparisons with famous outlaws, they were now wanted in two states, and a reward of $1,000 was being offered for the gang's leaders. We can only speculate on what the gang was planning, but the sudden shift from being more dangerous than Jesse James to not existing at all would only buy them time. Certainly there was much exaggeration about the gang's exploits, but real crimes had been committed with real witnesses. Dismissive news stories would not change the situation in Fayette County. In an attempt to avoid capture, the gang split into smaller groups and spent the next several weeks crossing back and forth over the Pennsylvania–West Virginia border.

The tactic proved unsuccessful for gang member William Turner. Sheriff Jackson of Preston County had formed a posse to capture any of the outlaws who passed into his jurisdiction. The group managed to find Turner alone in a house near the state line. Outnumbered, Turner surrendered without a fight. This was a bit of a surprise given his reputation. Several years earlier, he had been in a fight with two blacksmiths in Greene County, Pennsylvania. Turner was shot six times and still managed to beat both men. He had also been identified in a recent robbery and beating near Haydentown. Preston County authorities had identified Turner as one of the gang members who had robbed farms in their area. Turner was taken to prison but was quickly out on bond. More importantly, he decided to take advantage of his situation. Since he was the first member of the gang to be arrested since its explosion in the press, he had the opportunity to make a deal with the authorities. For the dismissal of some of the charges against him, Turner agreed to help hunt the Cooleys.

While the situation with Turner was unfolding across the state line, the Cooleys were back to their usual tricks near Smithfield. On February 15, Frank and Jack Cooley and Jack Ramsey stole food from the farm of Daniel Sutton. This time, perhaps inspired by the events in Preston County, the local citizens decided to fight back. A posse of almost 100 men tracked the trio of thieves to a coal pit. Despite their enormous advantage, their bravery soon faltered. As the posse approached the pit, they heard a noise coming from inside (assumed to be the click of a firearm). Almost in unison, the entire posse fled. A few moments later, the gang members casually walked out of the pit carrying their stolen goods. Though the posse proved ineffective, Sheriff McCormick was more successful. That same afternoon in Fairchance, he caught up with two other members of the gang. He managed to arrest Dick Cooley and Sam Yeager. Both were charged with robbery and attempted murder and were sent to the Uniontown jail. Days later, local papers reported that the sheriff had assembled his own posse of 15 deputies and former gang member William Turner. They would depart from Uniontown to hunt the outlaws. Sheriff McCormick and his counterparts in West Virginia coordinated their efforts. Together, they formed what they called a "circle of death" around the Cooley Gang. At the height of the search, the total number involved would reach 150 men.

McCormick and his allies had success almost immediately. On February 23, only two days after the posse set out, they captured a former Cooley associate named Bill Robinson. Robinson had fled to Greene County about a month before, hoping to avoid detection. He began to talk almost immediately, claiming that the gang was accused of crimes that it had not committed. Robinson had a falling out with Frank over Lyda Pastorious, which resulted in his near hanging at the hands of the outlaw. The altercation happened at Wesley Sisler's house. Sisler had allowed Pastorious to live with his family. Whatever happened, the Cooleys made Robinson dig his own grave and then let him dangle from a noose until he was unconscious. However, the two allegedly reconciled later. Despite this, Robinson described the Cooley boys as "chicken thieves" and said they were as "harmless as a fox." The gang was allegedly "frightened out of its senses" but knew the mountains well and could evade capture. Robinson was sent to the Uniontown jail with the others, though they were having difficulty in charging him with a crime.

When Jack Ramsey learned that their former friend William Turner was helping the sheriff, he sent an intermediary to him to convey his feelings. The man told Turner that Jack Ramsey was going to shoot him on sight. Turner sent the man back, indicating that he would do the same. Neither would get the chance. Turner still had to stand trial for robbing Abram Lowe in Fayette County the previous year. He was convicted on March 7, and the following day, Dick Cooley went to trial. He was also convicted of highway robbery and attacking Bill Robinson, partially based on Robinson's testimony. Testimony given by Lyda Pastorious was apparently also used against him, though it was not what she had intended. Dick received a two-year sentence.

Another member of the gang who had been trapped in the "circle of death" was Rufus Meyers. Meyers surrendered without a fight and was tried and convicted in early April. Meyers seemed to feel remorse over the accidental murder of Yost in Preston County, West Virginia, and admitted his guilt. He also named Frank Cooley and Sam Yeager as accomplices. This provided authorities with solid testimony to use against both men. Once the testimony was made public, however, several of the rewards offered for members of the gang were withdrawn by community leaders and the Georges Township School Board. It was felt that they were no longer necessary.

On some level, the local leaders were probably correct. The gang was now under intense pressure and, though its members attempted to hide it publicly, was becoming increasingly desperate. The Cooleys' next scheme was evidence of such desperation. According to contemporary reports, Frank and his friends decided to attempt a much larger robbery than they had ever tried before. They were going to hold up the New York and Philadelphia express (on the Baltimore & Ohio Railroad) near Layton Station on the evening of June 12. There was $186,000 onboard the train when it left Pittsburgh at 9:30 that evening. The men would either flag down the train so that they could board it or derail it by sabotaging the tracks. Unfortunately

CAPTURED AT LAST

Jack Cooley Fatally Shot While In the Act of Committing a Robbery.

HE DIED SATURDAY.

Thomas Collier's Spring House in Georges Township the Scene of the Shooting.

The Curious Manner In Which the Famous Young Desperado Met His Death—A Gun Arranged to Go Off When the Door of the Spring House Was Opened—A Musket Load of Buckshot In the Abdomed Did the Work—Cooley Lived Until Saturday

A headline from the *Republican Standard* announcing the death of Jack Cooley in 1892. *Courtesy of the Library and Archives Division, Senator John Heinz Pittsburgh Regional History Center.*

for the Cooleys, someone tipped off the railroad and the sheriff. Sheriff McCormick assembled a posse and stationed them near tracks at Layton Station. Six members of the Cooley Gang, including Frank and Jack Cooley and Jack Ramsey, were en route to the ambush when they were warned about the sheriff. They abandoned their plans and turned back. After the train passed safely, McCormick and his men attempted to catch the gang before they reached the mountains, but they were unsuccessful.

A critical blow was dealt to the gang on July 21, though not by law enforcement. Frank and Jack Cooley and Jack Ramsey had set out early that morning to rob the milk house of Thomas Collier, which was located near Fairchance. It was only three miles from their father's home. The three men thought they would just break in, take what they wanted and go home, as they had done on other farms. What they did not know was that Collier had grown tired of being robbed. Someone (probably the Cooleys) had broken into his milk house several times in the previous months. To prevent further loss, Collier decided to set a trap. He rigged a rifle to fire if the door was forced open. It would be Jack Cooley who approached the door and opened it. Before he could react, the shot struck him in the abdomen. Jack reeled backward and fell to the ground. His brother and Jack Ramsey dropped their revolvers, which were later found at the scene, and picked him up. The trio covered the agonizing three miles back to the Cooley homestead as quickly as possible.

When they reached their childhood home, Lute Cooley wanted to send for a doctor because he believed the wounds were serious. Frank, on the other hand, thought that Jack would be okay and was afraid that the sheriff and deputies would come for them if a doctor was summoned. Jack lingered in pain throughout the following day while Frank and his father remained at odds. Around midnight, Jack lost consciousness and Frank relented. Lute went to get Dr. Holbert, but when he arrived, it was clear that nothing could be done. Jack died around 4:00 a.m. A distraught Lute Cooley went into Fairchance the following morning to procure a coffin. He related the details of Jack's demise to the citizens whom he encountered.

Local politicians speculated that Jack's death would spell the end of the gang. Deputies were sent to arrest Frank Cooley and Jack Ramsey at Lute's home, but the two had already left. Jack was to be buried in Smithfield, and rumors circulated that Frank, Jack Ramsey and the rest of the gang would accompany the coffin to its resting place fully armed. They did not attend the funeral, however, and Sheriff McCormick's men monitored the entire procession. Instead, they allegedly watched from a distant hillside through a telescope. Newspapers reported that over five hundred curious people showed up to watch the funeral services, noting that it was the largest such procession ever held in Georges Township. It is impossible to determine how many of the attendees were family friends and how many were only spectators.

A sketch of Jack Cooley from the *Republican Standard* in 1892. *Courtesy of the Library and Archives Division, Senator John Heinz Pittsburgh Regional History Center.*

Contrary to what the authorities expected, the gang seemed to become more active after Jack's death. They also seemed to be turning on their friends. The day after the funeral, six members of the gang stormed into Wesley Sisler's house fully armed. The gang had normally been welcomed there, and Sisler had even been tarred and feathered on one occasion by members of the community for harboring the outlaws. This time, however, they drove the man out of his home and assaulted Lyda Pastorious. By this point, Lyda had given birth to a child, whom she would later acknowledge as belonging to Frank. Details on that evening are sparse, so it is not clear exactly what triggered the attack. It is assumed that Frank Cooley was one of the men. Sisler ran three miles into Fairchance to call Sheriff McCormick. He told him that if he could round up a posse, he could capture the gang at his house. McCormick took no action. Whatever the cause of the incident, it appears that Lyda and Frank quickly reconciled. When a newspaper reporter attempted to interview her in early August, she acknowledged that she was the "common law wife" of Cooley, despite being only twenty-two, and went on to say, "He is not half as black as he is painted, and he hasn't committed half of the crimes charged against him." Cooley's Queen went on to tell the reporter that she would not talk about Frank or the boys and sent the man on his way.

Around the same time, Ed Rankin, described in the press as a "new recruit" to the gang, managed to get himself arrested. Rankin had stolen thirty-two sheep and brought them into town for sale. He was going to use the money to go to Chicago. It seems that Rankin was probably just an occasional acquaintance of the Cooleys, but that was enough for the scandal-hungry newspapers to link him to the outlaws. Together, the two stories were enough to make the school board of Georges Township offer another reward—$750 for the capture of Frank Cooley.

In an attempt to deter would-be bounty hunters, the gang made it widely known that it was going to come after anyone who had opposed it or turned it in to the authorities. A train conductor named Tom Woods managed to evade the gang's wrath in late July when its members came looking for him on a stopped freight train near Fairchance. Woods had apparently revealed the gang's location to the sheriff two weeks earlier. Though Woods escaped harm, the Cooleys made it clear that they would be back. Uniontown councilman W.C. McCormick feared that he had been targeted by the gang as well. Just after Jack's funeral, he was awakened late at night to the sound of stones bouncing off the side of his house. When he opened the window to see who was responsible, shots rang out. The bullets missed and the councilman escaped harm, but he was frightened that the Cooleys would assassinate him for speaking against them.

Within days, Frank and the gang attempted to rob the paymaster of the Wynn Coke Works. The paymaster was notified by someone in advance that he might be a target. On that particular day, he took his usual route into Uniontown to draw money from the bank ($2,000). The Cooley Gang had planned to ambush him on the road as he returned to the works, which was about halfway between Uniontown and Fairchance. Instead, the paymaster took the train to Fairchance and then traveled by back roads to the works, avoiding the bandits altogether. After a long wait at the planned ambush site, the frustrated gang gave up and walked onto the Longhead farm. They used the Longhead family's chickens for target practice.

In the last few days of July, both Sheriff McCormick and Constable Frank Campbell of Connellsville led groups of armed men into the mountains to chase the gang but had little success. Western Pennsylvania newspapers were printing daily updates on the situation in Fayette County and made the gang appear almost untouchable. Tales of the Cooleys' exploits kept rolling in. Some tales were mere rumors, such as the story that the gang fled to Texas or had died drinking stolen milk that had been poisoned. Unfortunately for the people of Fayette County, others were not. Another home invasion was perpetrated by the group on July 31. Late in the evening, the gang stormed into the home of William Smith, who lived just north of Smithfield, and tied him with ropes. The outlaws intimidated the women in the house into retrieving $1,600 worth of their valuables and cash. They left in the direction of Dunbar. On the morning of August 1, they returned to Fairchance. On the way, they crossed paths with some boys, described as barefoot urchins, picking berries. Frank Cooley coldly stole their harvest.

Little activity was reported over the course of the following week. Then something almost surreal occurred. On the evening of Sunday, August 7, the Cooley Gang decided to go to church. Frank and his friends entered the Methodist church in Smithfield during an 8:00 p.m. service. Before walking through the door, the outlaws took a few moments to comb their hair and brush the dirt off their clothes. They entered wearing pistols in their belts but carried no rifles. Two members of the gang stood by the door and would not allow anyone in or out. The congregation recognized the men and anxiously waited for something to happen. Nothing did. Frank and the others sat down. When the service was over, Frank put money in the donation box, and the gang members mounted their horses and rode away.

Over the next two weeks, it was quiet in Fayette County. During this time, the Cooley Gang allegedly committed several robberies over the border near Kingwood, West Virginia. However, some Fayette County officials thought the gang was not responsible for those crimes and had actually fled to Westmoreland County instead. On August 21, the *Pittsburg Dispatch* ran a story about Dr. W.A. Longanecker, who had been called to check on Lyda Pastorious a few days earlier. The doctor's home had been robbed earlier that year and a variety of items were taken, including his bedclothes. When the doctor arrived to treat Lyda, he realized that the sheets and blankets on her bed were his own. When he was finished treating her, he gathered up his stolen belongings and started to leave. Lyda claimed that they were a gift from a friend, but that did not deter the doctor, who sternly told Lyda that her friend was a thief. Longanecker got into his buggy and rode off.

After almost a month of relative inactivity, the gang resurfaced on September 8 in Masontown. In their usual fashion, the outlaws forced their way into the home of John A. Walters and bound and gagged all the terrified occupants. The initial sweep of the house turned up no money, so a hot oil lamp was held to Walter's feet until he revealed its location. The gang also threatened to cut his throat with a razor if he did not comply. When it was over, the Cooley Gang walked away with $200, a wristwatch, a revolver and fine clothing. The gang's next target would also become their most well-known victim.

Sixty-two-year-old Jacob Prinkey was a successful farmer who lived at Gibbon's Glade in Wharton Township. He had made it into the newspaper early in of 1892, well before his encounter with the Cooleys, because of an apparently false report that he had been swindled out of $2,000 by a conman. Prinkey denied the story in early April, explaining that it was his brother in Springfield Township who had been swindled. It was clear, however, by the way the articles were written, that Prinkey was indeed wealthy. One article even quoted a neighbor who had at one time seen a large trunk full of money in the Prinkey home. One can reasonably assume that someone connected to the Cooleys read these articles, which resulted in Prinkey being added to their list of potential targets.

When the Cooley Gang began scouting the area around Prinkey's house in mid-September, they failed to (or perhaps did not care to) hide their presence. Prinkey noticed them lurking around the edges of his property and was aware that they spent at least one night in an abandoned building on his land. As a result, Prinkey quietly removed the money from his home and deposited it in a bank in Uniontown. His family also kept their firearms loaded, expecting trouble in the near future. Late in the evening on Saturday, September 24, that trouble arrived. The members of the Prinkey family were sitting in their house when they heard footsteps on the front porch. Jacob's son grabbed his revolver just as the door burst open. As the five outlaws entered the house, he fired two shots. One grazed one of the masked intruders, causing a minor wound and briefly igniting his clothing. The other man was struck in the torso and dropped to the floor. For a moment, the robbers hesitated and then turned and carried their wounded friend back out on the porch. The younger Prinkey had managed to shoot Frank Cooley.

While the rest of the gang carried their wounded friend out, Jacob went for his rifle. He was about to fire as the men rushed back into his house, but he was afraid that he would hit his son accidentally. Jack Ramsey pounced on Jacob while the others wrestled with his son. The gang managed to disarm them and tied both men to chairs. The women were forced to make a poultice out of bread and milk and apply it to Cooley's wound. Once the wound was wrapped, the gang looted the house. Not realizing that Prinkey's money was now in a bank, they were disappointed to discover that he had only twenty dollars in cash. The gang also took jewelry and clothing to supplement their score. When they finished, they headed off into the night, carrying their wounded leader with them.

The next morning, Prinkey was able to confirm the identity of his attackers. Just outside his house, he found a deck of cards that was dropped by the robbers. The name of one of the members of the Cooley Gang, Sam Yeager (who was out of prison), was written on the deck. A few steps later, Prinkey discovered a small club with Frank Cooley's name etched into it. On September 26, Prinkey traveled to Uniontown to report the crime. Frank Cooley had survived his wounds but had no idea how little time he had left. The Cooley Gang was about to meet its end.

George Fisher was a United States Secret Service detective. He had been assigned to Fayette County to pursue individuals who were illegally manufacturing moonshine. After having some success with his stated mission, Fisher quietly began to track the movements of the Cooley Gang. He learned that throughout September, Frank and various members of the gang visited Lute Cooley's home every Sunday and stayed for the afternoon. After a month of observation, he felt it was time to strike. Fisher quietly notified Sheriff McCormick and Frank Pegg, the head of a posse hired by W.W. Laughead, one of the Cooleys' wealthy victims. Setting out before dawn, the men stealthily gathered in the woods outside the Cooley homestead. Deputy Sheriff Allebaugh and Fairchance policeman Milt Hartley also joined the party. Around noon, the posse watched Frank Cooley and Jack Ramsey come up the road and enter the house. The decision was made to let Frank and Jack relax and let their guard down.

According to the first newspaper accounts, late in the afternoon, around 5:00 p.m., Frank and Jack emerged from the house and casually walked across the yard to the stumps of some freshly cut trees. The outlaws sat down with their backs against the stumps to relax in the sun. Both had their Winchester rifles at their sides. Sheriff McCormick gave his signal, and the posse crept toward the two men. Suddenly, a dog began to bark, alerting Frank and Jack to the sheriff's presence. Both men opened fire, initially from a seated position. The posse returned a volley of their own. As the outlaws were turning to run away, a bullet struck Frank in the heart, killing him instantly. Ramsey, who was faster than Frank, took off at full speed toward the Cooley home and then past it. Members of the posse were unable to catch him.

A few days after the shooting, Sheriff McCormick recounted a slightly different, more dramatic version of the story. It was also a version that made him sound more heroic in an attempt to counteract the criticism he had received for allowing the gang to operate for so long. The article opened with a lengthy paragraph emphasizing the bravery of the sheriff. It also failed to mention George Fisher and the posse assembled by Frank Pegg. The sheriff stated that when they ambushed the two bandits outside the Cooley home, Jack Ramsey was looking out through a field glass and Frank Cooley was holding a coat and a large pound cake. The two appeared to be heading off into the woods when they spotted the sheriff less than fifty feet away. The sheriff claimed that he said, "Boys, we've got you. You might as well give up. Throw up your hands." Cooley and Ramsey turned and ran immediately and, after about twenty-five feet, stopped and fired at the posse. Cooley allegedly fired two shots directly at the sheriff. In the sheriff's account, Cooley carried two pistols instead of a rifle. As Frank began to turn, the fatal bullet struck him. McCormick, now only five feet away, told him to throw up his hands, so he dropped the revolver in his right hand and raised it. The other pistol was still in his left hand as he slumped against a tree. The sheriff repeated his demand, but Cooley claimed that he could not. Realizing that he was now helpless, the sheriff stepped closer and said, "Frank, I'm sorry that it had to happen this way." Cooley allegedly replied, "You're not to blame George. You did your duty." He died thirty seconds later. The sheriff went on to emphasize the fact that Cooley was not a coward.

It is clear that the sheriff's account differs in some details from those that were initially reported. If Cooley had indeed been shot through the heart, it is unlikely that he had any type of conversation with the sheriff because he probably died almost instantly. Then again, newspapers of that era were known for their frequent mistakes and skewering of facts, so both accounts of Cooley's death could contain misinformation. Certainly the sheriff's account was meant to enhance his reputation, but it also provided more detail and was correct in the fact that Cooley was carrying pistols. The truth was probably somewhere between the two accounts. Either way, Frank Cooley was no longer a threat to Fayette County.

Now, the most pressing concern for the sheriff and his men was tracking Jack Ramsey. If Ramsey was brought in, the gang would truly be finished. Frank's death emboldened those who had previously lived in fear of the gang, and the very next morning, a tip came in placing Ramsey at a farm only a mile outside Fairchance. The sheriff's brother, Milt McCormick, received the information. He took A.J. Hicks and the Reverend J.L. Hunter with him to investigate. As the three men approached the farm, they spotted Ramsey, who immediately began to run. Milt and his companions caught up with Ramsey in a dry creek bed. Realizing that he could not escape, Ramsey hid

The graves of Frank and Jack Cooley in Smithfield, Pennsylvania. *Courtesy of Chris Lilley.*

his guns and moved away from them. Milt, with guns drawn, shouted that he would kill Ramsey if he attempted to resist. Ramsey allegedly replied, "Don't shoot Milt. I haven't any gun. I can't hurt anybody." Milt and his helpers handcuffed Ramsey and marched him back into town, where crowds gathered on Main Street to watch him pass.

Crowds had also made their way out to the Cooley homestead to get a look at Frank's body. It is estimated that over one thousand people made the trek out of curiosity. During his short life, Frank Cooley had become a household name in Fayette County and much of western Pennsylvania and West Virginia. He earned his reputation through theft, intimidation and violence. But Frank eventually reaped what he had sown. He was buried next to his brother Jack in Smithfield. Reverend Conway held the service for over two hundred mourners. Most were relatives.

Over the next few weeks, arrest warrants were issued for other members of the gang, the Cooley family and other associates of the outlaws. Jack Ramsey was brought to trial, convicted of multiple crimes including the Prinkey robbery and sentenced to nineteen years in prison. Being the most well known of the surviving members of the gang, he bore the brunt of the public's wrath. Two other longtime gang members—Charlie David and William Martin—were arrested and charged. Both men received five-and-a-half-year sentences. Sam Yeager turned state's evidence and was given a reduced sentence of eighteen months in a workhouse in exchange for his testimony. In a second wave of trials, Fayette County prosecutors went after family and friends who had received stolen property from the Cooley Gang. Lyda Pastorious was an obvious target. Since she had a small child (fathered by Frank Cooley), the court only sentenced her to eighteen months in a workhouse, and she was forced to pay court costs. Lyda was allowed to keep the baby with her at the workhouse hospital ward while she served her sentence. On December 17, the elderly Lute Cooley was acquitted of all charges against him, while his wife, Harriet, and several daughters were convicted. In an act of mercy by the court, the women's sentences were suspended. The era of the Cooley Gang was over.

PITTSBURGH'S EARLIEST BANK HEIST

M organ Neville was the cashier for the Farmers' and Mechanics' Bank in Pittsburgh. He arrived for work at his usual time on the morning of April 7, 1818, to find the bank doors unlocked. He cautiously made his way inside to discover that the door to the vault was open. Realizing a robbery had occurred, Neville immediately sent for the bank directors. The men hurried to the building and frantically counted the contents of the vault to determine what was missing. Though the exact figure was never released, it is believed that the thieves may have taken as much as $100,000 worth of bank notes and between $3,000 and $9,000 worth of coins, gold and other valuables. Also missing was the gold medal that the U.S. Congress had given to Neville's grandfather, General Daniel Morgan, in 1790. General Morgan received the commendation for his heroism during the Revolutionary War at the Battle of Cowpens. The authorities were alerted to the break-in, and together they quickly narrowed down a list of potential suspects. Suspicion centered on two men who had recently arrived in the young city and were both known to have gambling debts. Joseph "Doc" Pluymart and Herman Emmons also had questionable reputations. By all appearances, Pluymart seemed to be a well-dressed gentleman, but in reality, he was something of a career criminal. Emmons had once owned a store in New York before turning to thievery. It is not known how he came to associate himself with Pluymart.

As authorities began to ask questions, some tips came in that supported their suspicions. The suspects were spotted in Pittsburgh the evening of the

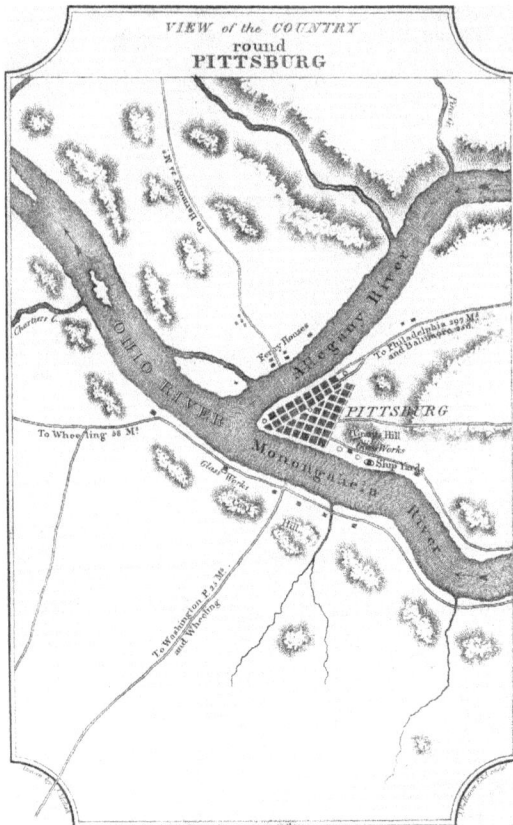

Pittsburgh in 1816. *Courtesy of the Library and Archives Division, Senator John Heinz Pittsburgh Regional History Center.*

robbery. More importantly, it was learned that the pair had purchased a small boat in the nearby town of Elizabeth along the Monongahela River. Pluymart and Emmons had requested that a false bottom be installed, presumably to hide their stolen loot. It was assumed that the thieves would then make their escape down the Ohio River. What the authorities and bank officials could not initially figure out, however, was how the pair got a copy of the vault key. No copies of the key were missing, so it was thought that the pair might have had some inside help. But thorough questioning of all those who had access to the vault keys made that scenario seem unlikely. The truth would only be learned after Emmons confessed.

Pluymart and Emmons never gained access to the vault keys. Instead, they managed to construct their own key by taking precise measurements of the vault's keyhole. While the pair was casing the bank before the robbery, they noticed that the night watchman left the key to the back door of the bank hanging visibly near the door of his small watch-box or watch station. Night after night, Pluymart and Emmons observed the watchman go into the box, sit down with his feet near a small stove and relax. As the watchman drifted in and out of sleep, the thieves stealthily removed the key and entered the bank. They carefully measured the keyhole of the vault and then quietly snuck back outside. The door key was returned to the watchman's booth, and the pair slipped away. This infiltration was repeated four more times as the thieves perfected their measurements. At one point, Emmons discovered that fifty dollars had been accidentally left out on the counter, but Pluymart ordered him not to take it so they would not blow their cover. The pair's patience paid off, and they were able to enter the vault with their own makeshift key.

William Lecky, one of the directors, had already set off downriver looking for the pair when the authorities learned of the secret compartment in the boat. Though a rider was dispatched to give him the information, it is not clear when he received it. Lecky and his men caught up with Pluymart and Emmons on the river near Wheeling, West Virginia. He detained the men and searched their boat. Apparently, he found nothing. It is not known if any of the stolen money was still in the secret compartment at that time, but it was later learned that the thieves dumped $1,200 worth of notes over the side when Lecky's boat was approaching. Lecky had no grounds to arrest the men yet, so he let them continue down the river. He sent word to authorities in Cincinnati, Ohio, to detain and search the men again when they reached that city. Lecky also set out for Cincinnati with his men. While all that was transpiring, a second batch of men left Pittsburgh and headed down the Ohio to intercept the thieves. They traveled as quickly as possible without stopping to rest. Somewhere along the way, they passed Lecky and caught sight of Pluymart and Emmons thirty miles upriver from Cincinnati. The thieves were stopped, arrested and taken downriver to the Cincinnati jail.

While Pluymart and Emmons were being followed down the Ohio River, the directors offered a reward for their apprehension and the return of the stolen money. In the days before modern banking insurance and regulation, such a financial loss could cripple a bank and destroy its reputation. Recovery of the money was vital to the bank's survival. The initial reward, offered on April 17, was $500 for the capture of the two men and $1,000 if the money was returned with them. By April 24, the reward had been raised to $1,000 and $3,000 respectively. The directors were unaware at that time that the pair was already in a Cincinnati jail. Word of their arrest would not reach Pittsburgh for another four days. Pittsburgh authorities initiated the process of extradition to bring the thieves back for trial, only to have their transport delayed by a dispute over the process.

While judges and newspapers debated the issue, Pluymart and Emmons decided to take advantage of the situation. While they waited in jail, they came up with a plan to escape. The surviving details of their breakout are vague, but it is known that they both made it out of the prison. Pluymart managed to elude the search parties that set out after them. Emmons was not as lucky. At some point during the escape (or possibly during the capture), his arm was broken. Emmons was caught and taken back to the jail. In early June, he was transported back to Pittsburgh to stand trial.

When Emmons reached the city, he was given the opportunity to cut a deal. He agreed to show prosecutors the hiding place of the money and reveal all details of the crime in exchange for no jail sentence. The bank supported such a deal if it meant that it could recover the money. Emmons confessed that after the break-in, the two men had stopped at a large rock below the spot where the Beaver River empties into the Ohio. There, in a small natural cave, they stashed the bank notes and some of the money.

Emmons was put onboard a boat at night and made to lead the authorities to the hiding place, which was about thirty-seven miles downriver. When they reached the spot, the bank notes and about $1,800 worth of silver were concealed in the small space. The notes had sustained some water damage, but the vast majority of the stolen money had been recovered. One notable thing was missing—General Morgan's medal. It was noted that Emmons genuinely appeared surprised that the medal was not with the rest of the money. He guessed that Pluymart might have pocketed the medallion when they were hiding their loot in the dark. Otherwise, the men had only taken small amounts of the money for personal expenses and planned to return for the rest of it later.

While this was going on, "Doc" Pluymart was stealthily making his way north back into the state of New York. He was approaching the Canadian border in early June when authorities managed to trap him near Ogdensburg. Pluymart was traveling in disguise and initially attempted to talk his way out of trouble. The New York authorities were not fooled and held him for questioning. After a quick search, they discovered that he was transporting $700 worth of gold, $1,500 worth of bank notes from the Farmers' and Mechanics' Bank and nearly $3,000 worth of bank notes from other banks west of the Appalachians. General Morgan's medal was not among his possessions. He would later imply that it had already been sold. A New York magistrate charged Pluymart with robbery and sent him to jail to await extradition.

THE BANK OF PITTSBURGH
is situated on the s. w. corner of Market and
Third streets.

PRESIDENT,
William Wilkins.
DIRECTORS,

George Anshutz, Jun.	Thos. Cromwell
Nicholas Cunningham	John Darragh
William Hays	Wm. McCandless
James Morrison	John M. Snowden
Craig Ritchie (Canonsbr'g)	George Allison
James Brown (baker)	T. P. Skelton

CASHIER,
Alexander Johnston, Jun.

Open daily from 9 o'clock a. m., till 3 p. m.,
except Sunday, Fourth of July, Christmas and
Fast days. Discount day, Wednesday. Capital, $600,000. Shares, $50 each. Dividends,
first Mondays in May and November.

THE FARMERS' AND MECHANICS' BANK
OF PITTSBURGH,

CASHIER,
George Poe, Jun.

Open daily from 9 o'clock a. m. till 3 p. m.,
except Sunday, Fourth of July, Christmas and
Fast days. Discount day, Thursday.
Is situated on the north side of Third, between Market and Wood streets.

PRESIDENT,
John Scull,
DIRECTORS,

William Eichbaum, Jun.	William Leckey
John Ligget	Jacob Negley

Richard Robinson	John Robinson
John Hannon	Matthias Evans
Mark Stackhouse	Thomas Perkins
George Miltenberger	Robert Peebles.

CASHIER,
George Luckey.

Open daily, except Sundays, 1st Jan. 4th July, Christmas day, and Fast days, from 9 o'clock
A. M. till 3 P. M.—Discount day, Tuesday.—
Capital $450,000.—Shares $50 each.—Dividends on first Mondays n May and November.
Notes for discount in either of the banks,
must be deposited before 3 o'clock of the evening preceding the discount day.

THE PITTSBURGH AND GREENSBURGH
TURNPIKE COMPANY.

PRESIDENT,
William Wilkins.

MANAGERS,

Wm. B. Foster	Thomas Sampson
Jacob Negley	Ephraim Pentland
Dunning M'Nair	—— Patterson
Wm Caven	James Irwin
Wm. Fullerton	Wm. Hindman
Tobias Painter	Abraham Horbach

TREASURER,
William Friedt
G 4

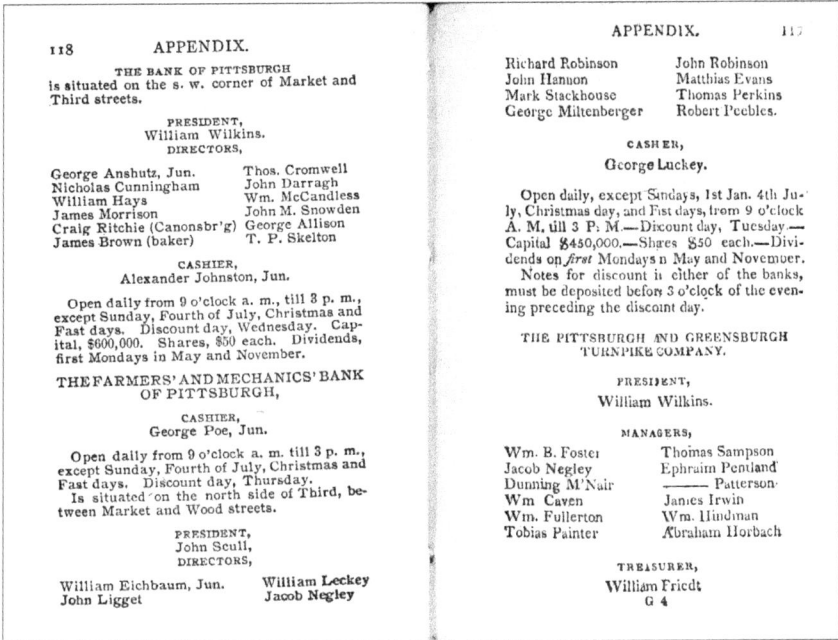

Pages from the 1815 Pittsburgh City Directory advertising the Farmers' and
Mechanics' Bank. *Courtesy of the University Archives and Special Collections at the Gumberg
Library, Duquesne University.*

The matter was seemingly resolved. But two nights later, Pluymart seized
another opportunity to escape. There was a jailbreak, apparently with help
from the outside, where Pluymart was being held. He managed to get out of
the prison with two other men and flee into the night. Immediately, a posse
was assembled to track the escaped men. Pluymart and his two accomplices
only covered fifteen miles before they were apprehended again and were
returned to Ogdensburg.

The record becomes somewhat unclear at that point as to Pluymart's
whereabouts. It would be presumed that he was transported back to
Pittsburgh for trial, but most sources place his trial nearly a decade later in
1828. Some imply that he escaped yet again in the interim and remained
on the run. At some point, he was recaptured yet again and returned to
Pennsylvania.

In Pittsburgh, Pluymart was convicted and sentenced to serve three years
in prison as well as pay a fine of $1,000. Finally, the matter seemed settled—
until Pluymart escaped again! Almost no details of his final escape from

the Western Penitentiary have been passed down, quite possibly because of embarrassment on the part of prison officials. Numerous attempts were made to recapture Pluymart, but he always slipped away. Finally, Pennsylvania governor John Andrew Schulze broke the cycle of capture and escape by issuing Pluymart a full pardon. Pluymart was still on the run at the time, so it is not known how or when he received the news. Critics of the governor claimed that both men were Freemasons and that Schulze granted the man's freedom out of a sense of brotherhood. Schulze was indeed a Mason, but it has not been confirmed that Pluymart was ever a member of the order. It is more likely that the accusation stemmed from the anti-Masonic sentiment of the day. The governor's true intentions will never be known. However, Joseph Pluymart became one of the few individuals who has ever robbed a bank, repeatedly escaped from prison and walked away clean.

The Farmers' and Mechanics' Bank did not fare as well. Its reputation was tarnished, and rumors of dishonesty circulated widely. The institution had difficulty functioning in Pittsburgh and soon found that its credit had been destroyed even with international banks. Starting in 1819, the bank was forced to gradually retire all of its notes. By 1821, the bank found itself unable to pay the taxes that it owed the state and, by default, forfeited its charter. The state legislature ordered the bank to liquidate its remaining assets to pay off its debts in 1825 and then to shut its doors.

THE MAUG "MOB"

Early in the morning of May 3, 1932, Ross Township police constable Vernon Porter Moses stopped a suspicious vehicle that was traveling north on Perry Highway. The vehicle was near the Keating Car Barns, which housed off-service trolleys. Constable Moses was wary of the vehicle, which carried three men, because of a string of car barn robberies that had occurred in the Greater Pittsburgh area in recent months. A man named William Lal was walking nearby and watched Moses approach the car. It was clear to Lal that the men in the vehicle were becoming belligerent and agitated with Moses's questions. For a moment, the constable looked up at Lal and shouted for him to get additional help. Lal turned and started off to find another officer. He did not get far when he heard gunfire ring out. Lal returned to the scene of the stop only to see the suspicious car speeding away and Constable Moses bleeding out on the ground. The constable would not survive his wounds. Though the murder remained unsolved for weeks, persistent detectives eventually linked the killing to the Maug Gang, often referred to as the "Maug Mob" in the press.

The Maug Gang was a small-time outfit of thieves and occasional bootleggers that operated briefly in the early 1930s in southwestern Pennsylvania. It was named after its leader, John Maug, who was only twenty-one years old at the time of the murder of Constable Moses. It was he who had pulled the trigger and ended the lawman's life. Maug's closest associates were Edward Turpack and Charles Moyer. They were the other two men in the car at the time of the shooting. The trio was responsible

The mug shot of John Maug. *Authors' collection.*

for most of the robberies and other crimes attributed to the gang. Other alleged associates of the gang included Wallace and Roscoe Biggert, John Flaherty, Herman Moulden, Daniel Flory, Thomas Byrnes, Edna Friedel (Maug's sister), Alexander and Eleanor Stemmler and Maug's girlfriend, Gladys Jackson.

The early crimes and exploits of the Maug Gang are not well documented and details are lacking, but they did seem to target companies involved in transportation. They stole payrolls and trolley fares in the months before the killing of Vernon Moses. The gang members would later admit (after their arrest) to robbing the main office of the Pittsburgh Motor Coach Company, as well as the Ingram and Bunker Hill Car Barns. During these robberies (and others that the gang did not admit to), they fired at and injured at least two other police officers. In one case, they shot and wounded Constable Carl Hildebrand of Reserve Township during a shootout in St. Peter's Cemetery on Mount Troy Road. In addition to the quick cash heists, the gang occasionally trafficked in small amounts (compared to the large bootleggers) of alcohol in the last years of Prohibition.

For the remainder of 1932, police and detectives from various departments started to piece together the clues that would identify Maug and his friends as the killers. In early July, Chester Zygello, chief of the

The Maug "Mob"

The mug shot of Edward Turpack. *Authors' collection.*

Sharpsburg Police, picked up Turpack and Moyer on unrelated charges of theft. Though the two were eventually released, he started to build a case for connecting them to other crimes. Some Pittsburgh Police detectives were also busy linking the gang to recent robberies and to the Moses killing. Before the end of the year, the father-and-son detective team of Frank and Thomas Morgan was ready to make its move. Most of the gang was arrested at their makeshift headquarters, an old rooming house on North Lincoln Avenue. By January 1933, the Maug Mob was headed to court. All three men confessed to the previously mentioned robberies after their arrest, but none admitted to the murder.

On January 23, Maug, Turpack and Moyer were in criminal court. The room was under heavy guard because of rumors that friends of the gang might attempt to "shoot their way out." When the charge of murder was addressed, Moyer turned on Maug, identifying him as the gunman. The testimony led to a falling-out between the two men. Moyer had also disclosed (before the trial) that the gang dumped six guns, including the .45 that was used in the murder, in the Monongahela River after the killing. According to newspaper reports, authorities were able to recover most of the weapons with powerful electromagnets. The five pistols that were recovered were presented in court, but none was a definite forensic match to the murder weapon. In what may have been an attempt for leniency, the three criminals eventually all confessed to having parts in the murder. It may have worked, because at sentencing the following day, Maug avoided the death penalty. Instead, he and Turpack were sentenced to life in prison plus 60 to 120 years. Moyer was given a 40- to 80-year sentence. All three were returned to the Allegheny County Jail for a brief time before being sent to Western Penitentiary on the North Side to serve their time.

Several of the gang's associates were also brought up on various charges for assisting with crimes. The evidence against the others was not nearly as conclusive. Herman Moulden fared the worst, receiving twenty to forty years for aiding in the robberies. Wallace Biggert was convicted and given five to ten years, and Roscoe Biggert was sentenced to time in a workhouse. Maug's girlfriend, Gladys Jackson, was given three years' parole for allegedly helping the gang to manufacture dynamite. The rest of Maug's friends were given suspended sentences or acquitted.

Almost immediately upon arrival at the penitentiary, Maug began to hatch a plan for Turpack and himself to escape. The pair allied themselves with two other inmates who were also desperate to be free of the confines of the prison. Freddie Prince, known as the "Pock-Marked Bandit," was serving time for robbery and killing a policeman in Ohio, and Theodore Joseph Geisler had been given a long sentence for robbery. Together, the four men began to subtly steal supplies from the prison to aid in their escape. On April 27, 1933, Maug and his allies put their carefully constructed plan into action. The men had all managed to create dummies to fill their bunks and hide their absence. The dummies were apparently left in their bunks when they were working in the yard. How this was possible is unclear, but the prison guards were later accused of negligence (and rumors of their complicity in the escape were also common). Initial reports said that the four men ate dinner with the rest of the inmates but found an opportunity to slip away when it was time to return to their cells. Geisler later revealed that they slipped away around 3:30 p.m. and did not return for the pre-dinner roll call. Instead, Maug and his friends stealthily maneuvered through the prison yard. Their goal was to reach the roof of the hospital and chapel. One of the criminals was carrying a rope made from cotton fibers and tape stolen from the prison weaving shop. At 9:00 p.m., guards checked the cells and reported all four men present. They had been fooled by the dummies (or chose to ignore them) and would not check the cells again until morning. Sometime over the night, probably between 3:00 and 4:30 a.m., the four inmates assembled pieces of scaffolding left outside into a makeshift ladder

A postcard from the early twentieth century depicting the Western Penitentiary. *Courtesy of the Library and Archives Division, Senator John Heinz Pittsburgh Regional History Center.*

to reach the roof of the chapel. They tied their rope to the bars outside an upper window near the outer wall of the prison and slid down over eighty feet to freedom. The only eyewitness to their escape was a newsboy who was on his way to pick up copies of the early morning paper for distribution. He reported seeing four men, wearing what appeared to be prison work clothes, hurrying down a street not far from the penitentiary.

A search was launched after 5:00 a.m. when guards discovered the dummies. By that time, the escapees had a substantial head start. Police immediately descended on the homes of Maug's sister, Edna Friedel, and his mother, Ada Rothermel. He was at neither location, but police did discover thirty-five gallons of alcohol at the Friedel home. Edna was arrested. After checking out all of the gang's known associates, the police were forced to acknowledge that the trail had gone cold. A $10,000 reward was offered for the capture of Maug and Turpack. Authorities hoped that the promise of cash would help to deliver the escapees to the law. Prince and Geisler, who went their own way after the jailbreak, were recaptured the next day by two policemen on the North Side.

Over the following months, numerous sightings of the escapees were reported to police. Some came from neighborhoods in Pittsburgh's east end, such as Point Breeze. Another placed them in an old stone quarry in Mifflin Township. A raid was launched at an old house in the Hill District because it was once a former hideout of the gang. They were not there. None of the leads panned out. Detectives followed what turned out to be a false lead into southern Ohio on May 22. After a full day of searching over thirty-five square miles, they returned to Pittsburgh empty-handed. At one point at the beginning of June, the trail led them to New York. Someone claiming to be Maug phoned the Brooklyn Police headquarters, though authorities did not reveal what he said. The call was traced to a phone booth outside a cigar store on Nostrand Avenue. When they investigated, the clerk at the cigar store said that a young man, about the age of twenty-one, had come in to ask for change to use the phone. He had no hat or jacket and looked a bit disheveled. The Brooklyn police believed that if Maug and Turpack were in New York, they may have been responsible for a recent street robbery where a man was killed.

In reality, Maug and Turpack were far from New York. After leaving Allegheny County, they fled in the opposite direction and ended up in Cleveland. On the way, they committed several hold-ups in Pittsburgh and the surrounding areas. The day of the escape, the men stole a car on Liverpool Street on the North Side. On May 5, they robbed a special officer of the Jones and Laughlin Steel Corporation, William Struck, at gunpoint. They took his pistol and blackjack. Maug and Turpack hid in an abandoned chicken coop on a farm in Carrick for several days. Police eventually raided the farm after a tip, but the outlaws had already left. Turpack struck again on May 9 on Baldwin Road. He approached Irene Dowling and Elmer Bomford after the couple had entered a car. He demanded that they get out, and when they refused, he fired a shot through the windshield. Turpack got in the back seat and forced them to drive to an old coal mine, where he left them bound and gagged. He took their money and the car. Seven days later, the outlaws held up a coffee shop, taking $300 from the register. The pair of outlaws then headed north. They reached Erie, Pennsylvania, on May 24 and stole a car off a dealer's lot. For more spending cash, they robbed a small store and then headed west.

By the end of May, Maug and Turpack were in the Cleveland suburb of Lakewood. Maug carefully selected his next target: a local Western Union telegraph office. On May 31, the two men stormed into the office and took $118. After the robbery, the thieves kept a low profile for several days. On June 16, Maug and Turpack decided to strike again. Strangely enough, instead of moving on to another target, they decided

BUREAU OF DETECTIVES
ALLEGHENY COUNTY, PITTSBURGH. PA.

May 19, 1933

$10,000 REWARD

TEN THOUSAND DOLLARS

By virtue of the following resolution:

At a meeting of the Board of Commissioners held today the following resolution was adopted and ordered spread upon the minutes of this meeting:

Whereas, John Maug and Edward John Turpac did escape from the Western Penitentiary on Thursday, April 27, 1933, and

NOW THEREFORE BE IT RESOLVED, that the County Commissioners of Allegheny County, pursuant to authority vested in them, do hereby authorize as follows:

$5,000.00 to any person causing the arrest or capture of John Maug, DEAD or ALIVE.

$5,000.00 to any person causing the arrest or capture of Edward John Turpac, DEAD or ALIVE.

The above rewards will be paid only by the County of Allegheny on certificate of the District Attorney of Allegheny County, that the person or persons claiming the reward are entitled thereto.

ESCAPE OF TWO CONVICTED MURDERERS FROM THE WESTERN PENITENTIARY, April 27, 1933, as follows:

Description of
John Maug:
Alias John William Maug

Convicted of murder, robberies and other felonies.

Age 21, looks 25, height 5 feet 7³⁴ inches, weight 140 pounds, build medium, hair chestnut, eyes blue, complexion medium or sallow.

Finger Print classification
31 1M 23
28 MO 18

Description of
Edward John Turpac:
Alias Andrew Turpac,
John Reno

Convicted of murder, robberies and other felonies.

Age 26, looks 28, height 5 feet 8¹⁴ inches, weight 144 pounds, medium build, hair black, eyes dark brown, complexion dark.

Finger Print classification
15 1 U 111 4
13 1 U 110 5

THESE MEN are DESPERATE, WELL ARMED and WILL SHOOT TO KILL.

Charles C. McGovern, W. D. Mansfield, and C. M. Barr, County Commissioners of Allegheny County, Pa., will pay the above reward.

Attest: Robt. Woodside, County Controller.

WIRE ALL INFORMATION TO

Andrew T. Park, *District Attorney* or George W. Murren, *Chief of County Detectives*
PITTSBURGH, PA.

This wanted poster appeared after John Maug and Edward Turpack escaped from Western Penitentiary in 1933. They were considered dangerous enough to warrant a $10,000 reward. *Authors' collection.*

to go back and rob the same Western Union office. This would prove to be their undoing.

The outlaws needed transportation to their destination, so they carjacked a cab driven by Norman Piccus. Pretending to be normal customers, Maug and Turpack suddenly drew their guns and bound and gagged Piccus in the back seat. Piccus later reported that the two struggled with driving the cab and following the directions to the office. The men dumped Piccus in a yard belonging to a Mrs. Kuhns. In an apparent lapse of judgment, the men did not realize that she would call the police. Maug and Turpack continued to the telegraph office. As they were exiting the cab, Detectives Edward Graske and Delmar Potts pulled up. They had responded to the call of Mrs. Kuhns, untied Piccus and still managed to get to the Western Union office at about the same time as the outlaws. The detectives jumped from their vehicle with guns drawn. Maug and Turpack hesitated only briefly and then decided to drop their weapons and surrender. They were taken to the police station for identification. It took nearly twelve hours before police in Cleveland verified the identities of the men through their fingerprints. After their identities were known, the $10,000 reward was divided among Graske, Potts, Piccus and Kuhns, though the officers were mandated to contribute their portion to the police retirement fund.

Initially, Maug and Turpack considered fighting extradition to Pennsylvania, but for unknown reasons, they changed their minds. They agreed to go without a fight if William Gaffney, the special investigator for Western Penitentiary, came and escorted them back. While the outlaws waited, they enjoyed a steak dinner courtesy of a *Pittsburgh Post-Gazette* photographer. Maug and Turpack had agreed to talk and stand for pictures in exchange for the meal. Gaffney arrived late in the evening on June 17 to secure the prisoners. Upon his return to western Pennsylvania, Maug received more disheartening news. His former girlfriend, Gladys Jackson, had quietly married a soldier named George Walker. She had ceased all contact with Maug after their arrest and was determined to leave her past behind.

Upon their return to the Allegheny County Jail, Maug and Turpack were held in the "home," which was a series of solitary confinement cells for prisoners who had committed behavioral infractions. Maug was placed in the same cell that had been inhabited by Paul Jaworski, leader of the Flathead Gang, during his incarceration. Later, they were moved back to Western Penitentiary. Maug had apparently not learned his lesson and once again plotted escape, but this time he would be caught before he got out. In

The Maug "Mob"

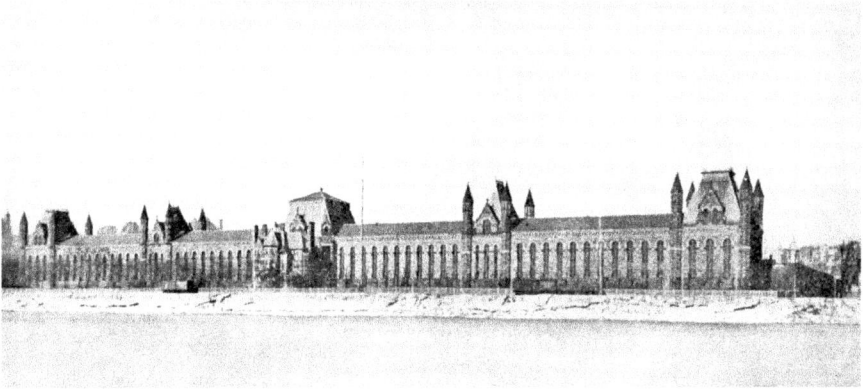

Western Penitentiary as seen from the Ohio River. *Courtesy of the Library and Archives Division, Senator John Heinz Pittsburgh Regional History Center.*

October 1934, an observant guard noticed a problem with the bars on Maug's cell. Upon closer inspection, he realized that they had been partially sawn through. Maug was kept under careful watch after the incident, and it was several years before he attempted another escape. Police discovered the plot in early March 1940 after another former inmate named Stephen "Mooch" Krenicky was arrested at the bus station in Pittsburgh. He had befriended Maug in prison while serving time for robbery and had subsequently been released. When the police picked him up, he was carrying plans for stealing dynamite and strategically placing it along the wall at Western Penitentiary. He was going to create a "door" for Maug to escape through. It is not known if Maug ever attempted to escape again. If he did, which is likely given his record, the details never went beyond the prison walls.

While Maug plotted escape, Turpack's lawyers issued a legal challenge to his life sentence. Because of the order in which Turpack was charged and convicted of his crimes, his lawyers argued that the life sentence was improperly applied. After a series of court appeals, the state Supreme Court agreed and eliminated the life sentence because of the technicality. Turpack continued to serve his other sentences for robbery and became a model prisoner. The warden and other evaluators were convinced of his reform, and after Turpack served nineteen years, Governor George Fine commuted his sentence. Turpack was released in May 1952 and moved to Cleveland to live with his sister.

A VIOLENT END TO A CRIME SPREE

S mall-time criminals Albert Feelo, Virgil Evarts and Kenneth Palmer all served time together in Rockview Penitentiary in central Pennsylvania during the 1930s. Little definitive information about their interactions during their incarcerations exists, but the three troublemakers seem to have forged some level of friendship. By 1941, all three men had been released from prison and decided to reconnect with each other. Their reacquaintance would ultimately prove disastrous for all.

The youngest of the three men, Feelo, was from the town of Republic in Fayette County and was twenty-six years old at the time. Thirty-three-year-old Kenneth Palmer was originally from the town of Volant in Lawrence County. The most experienced of the three men, he had been imprisoned for robbing a bank. Evarts, who hailed from Smithfield, Fayette County, was twenty-seven. In early September, the former convicts gathered in a bar in Uniontown. When the men had left prison, they had intended to find jobs and stay out of trouble. At some point during their casual meeting, their plans changed. It will never be known which of the three men suggested that they return to a life of crime. Maybe it was an idea revived from their days at Rockview. Perhaps they just could not readapt to life on the outside. In the end, their motivations would matter little. The three men were about to embark on a two-week crime spree that would capture headlines across western Pennsylvania.

Before launching into their crime spree, the trio made a quick trip to Detroit. Palmer had a wife in the city, and it is assumed that he visited her.

On the way back, the three men passed through Cleveland. While in that city, they acquired a new mode of transportation. The men returned to western Pennsylvania on Thursday, September 11, driving a stolen black 1939 Buick. They also had a plan. By targeting rural businesses and banks, the men hoped to avoid direct confrontation with the police. It was in the town of Farrell, Mercer County, where the men decided to strike first. The men stormed into the office of Francke & Co. Insurance that weekend to seize the money held in its safe. The armed criminals forced manager Albert Snyder to open the safe before tying him up, along with several female employees. Feelo, Evarts and Palmer got away with about $400 from the heist. It was not long before they were ready for their next crime.

On Monday night, September 15, the three thieves parked their car behind Rohrer's Gun Store in New Castle. After breaking in, the men took $100 from the register, but more importantly, they took firearms and ammunition. They left the building with twenty handguns and several rifles. Having the extra weapons would give them a little "insurance" for their next job, or so they thought. What the men did not know was that a New Castle city electrician, Rex Hughes, got a partial plate number from their car when it was suspiciously parked in the back alley. That number was turned over to local law enforcement after it became known that a robbery had occurred.

For the next three days, Feelo, Evarts and Palmer plotted their next score. This time, they were going for a larger payoff. On the afternoon of Friday, September 19, the three bandits traveled to Butler County. They pulled up in front of the Harrisville Bank shortly before it was set to close for the day. One of the men waited in the car (it is not clear which one) while the other two entered the bank with their weapons concealed. They walked up to the counter and asked the cashier for $2 worth of nickels. As the man was fulfilling their request, the barrels of handguns were thrust in his face. The robbers threatened to blow his brains out if he tried anything. The rest of the bank employees and a lone customer were forced to the floor and told to stay quiet. The robbers took at least $2,000 out of the register. Some of the early newspaper accounts stated that $3,000 was taken. While the robbery was in progress, an employee of a local lumber company walked into the bank. He was carrying a deposit of $350, which was immediately seized by the armed men. Once they had their money, the men charged out of the bank with guns still in hand and jumped into the waiting car, which sped down Route 8 and then turned off to the west.

Next to the bank was a hardware store owned by Arthur Brenneman. He had noticed the car idling in front of the bank and paused to watch from his window. Brenneman saw the armed men emerge and carefully committed their descriptions (as well as a description of their car) to memory. As they drove off, he called the police and told them everything he had seen. Police dispatchers immediately relayed all the information to local police departments. The license plate of the car matched the partial plate reported at the time of the gun store robbery. A couple traveling on West Pittsburg Road heard the announcement on their radio and looked ahead to see the getaway car racing past them toward Ellwood City. The couple pulled over and called the Ellwood City Police Department.

Chief Ernest Hartman received the call at the Ellwood City Station and took down the details. Then he grabbed a Thompson submachine gun, got into his patrol car and headed out to intercept the outlaws. Hartman proceeded to the Fifth Street Bridge and parked his car just across the span on the north side. He got out, Tommy gun in hand, and kept watch for the outlaws. The chief only waited a few minutes before the stolen Buick approached. After stepping out in the road to stop the car, Hartman demanded that the men exit the vehicle with their hands in the air. As Feelo, Evarts and Palmer stepped out of the car, it appeared that they were complying with the chief's orders. Suddenly, the three men drew their pistols and opened fire, discharging seventeen rounds in total. As bullets whizzed past him, Hartman kept his cool and raised his Tommy gun, unleashing a barrage of bullets at the three criminals. All three of the men were struck by bullets. Feelo took the most shots, having bullets pass through both lungs and his spine. Miraculously, not a single bullet had hit Hartman.

Evarts and Palmer dragged Feelo back into the car as they tried to return fire. The bleeding and wounded men floored it, trying to put as much distance between themselves and the chief as possible. Hartman returned to his patrol car, turned around and followed the outlaws south on Fifth Street. Citizens pointed out the direction the criminals had taken. In the meantime, an off-duty police officer named Edward Shaffer, who had witnessed the end of the shootout, hopped into the car of his friend James Pasta, and the two men joined in on the pursuit. They took a different route than the chief in an attempt to head off the escape car.

The wounded criminals turned onto the unpaved portion of Belton Road. Evarts, who had been shot in the shoulder, was behind the wheel. Due to his wound, he lost control of the vehicle near a bend, and the car went straight off the side of the road and down a ten-foot embankment, stopping when it ran into a tree. Evarts and Palmer staggered out of the wreckage and crawled back up to the road. The climb was difficult for Palmer because he had bullet wounds in both legs. The pair brandished their guns (Evarts had a rifle) and stopped the first car that came down the road. Angelo DeCarlo was the unlucky driver. In the passenger seat was Laura Kash, whose car had broken down farther up the road. DeCarlo had stopped to give her a ride. Now they were facing two armed and desperate criminals. Evarts demanded that the two exit the car, go down the embankment and carry the severely wounded Feelo back up and into DeCarlo's car. Before they could react, the car carrying Shaffer and Pasta screeched to a halt nearby. Both men got out of the car, but there was a problem. Shaffer did not have his gun. Now Evarts and Palmer had four hostages.

Evarts ordered Shaffer and Pasta to get Feelo, and the unarmed men reluctantly complied. Climbing down the embankment, they retrieved the outlaw and carried him to the back seat of DeCarlo's car. Shaffer was still in the back, and Palmer got into the passenger seat. Evarts laid his rifle across Palmer's lap as he walked around the car to the driver's side. Pasta was now standing just outside the car and saw his opportunity to act. He quickly yanked the rifle off Palmer's lap and pointed it at Evarts. Evarts froze briefly and then yelled for Palmer to get a handgun that he had stashed in the glove compartment. As Palmer went for the gun, Shaffer lunged over the seat and attempted to wrestle it out of his hands. Evarts started to move, so Pasta fired, shooting Evarts in the mouth. Evarts fell backward down the embankment and, incredibly, stood back up and headed toward the wrecked car to retrieve another gun. Pasta ran down the embankment and struck him in the head with the butt of the rifle. The blow was fatal.

Up at DeCarlo's car, Palmer had managed to grab a wrench that was lying on the floor of the vehicle and struck Shaffer in the head. What Palmer did not realize was that Laura Kash had also picked up a wrench. She snuck up behind him and slammed it down onto his head. As Palmer staggered in a daze, Shaffer recovered from the blow he received, and Pasta climbed back up the embankment. The two men beat Palmer into submission. Chief Hartman arrived on the scene as Palmer went down. As Hartman approached, he realized that Feelo had somehow retrieved a pistol and was preparing to fire a shot from the back seat. The chief easily disarmed the dying man.

Soon more police cars arrived, and the outlaws were taken to the hospital in Ellwood City. Evarts was dead on arrival, and Feelo only survived until the following morning. Inside the wrecked getaway car, police found plans for more robberies, as well as the rest of the stolen firearms. After Palmer was released from the hospital, he was tried and convicted for armed robbery.

A Violent End to a Crime Spree

He was given a twenty-year sentence and was returned to Rockview. He was released after serving four years. Hartman, Pasta, Shaffer and the others were recognized as heroes in the local community.

GLENN AND IRENE

Western Pennsylvania's Bonnie and Clyde

In 1929, two years before the notorious outlaws Bonnie and Clyde ever made the headlines, western Pennsylvania had its own criminal duo that terrorized the region. During their short career as an outlaw couple, Irene Crawford Schroeder and Walter Glenn Dague robbed numerous convenient stores and gas stations to fund a lifestyle they could not otherwise afford. The climax of their career (and what ultimately sent them to the electric chair) occurred when a pair of New Castle police officers attempted to stop them after a grocery store hold-up in Butler.

Before their less-than-infamous crime spree, Schroeder was living with her father. She had recently been divorced and was waitressing at a small West Virginia diner to support her four-year-old son Donnie. Dague supported his family (a wife and two sons) by selling insurance. In his spare time, Dague taught Sunday school and was a local Boy Scout leader. Though both were leading apparently normal lives, their meeting ultimately triggered a dramatic change. Their relationship began after a few chance encounters around the town of Wheeling. They first met when Schroeder, on her way to work, was almost hit by Dague's car. To amend for his inattentive driving, Dague drove the now dirty Schroeder to his house for her to clean up and change. Though their relationship did not necessarily begin in the most conventional fashion, they quickly became romantically involved.

The affair eventually enticed Dague to leave his small family, his work and everything else that grounded him in West Virginia. With Schroeder, he began to move around the Northeast looking for work. Dague worked odd jobs to help support his new flame and her young son. Somewhere amid these travels, the two started to rob gas stations and grocery stores to help sustain a comfortable lifestyle and perhaps add excitement to their otherwise mundane lives. Their robberies, which tended to be violent, took them across state lines into Ohio, Pennsylvania, Missouri and Tennessee and in their wake left countless witnesses who would later come back to haunt the pair. It was common practice for Glenn and Irene to hogtie store managers and employees and threaten them with bodily harm or death. Some of their targets included an A&P and numerous grocery stores in Cincinnati, a Kroger store and an independent furniture store in Toledo and grocery stores in Greensburg, Pittsburgh and Uniontown, Pennsylvania. Many of the owners and employees of these stores were later able to provide descriptions of the couple. The two also used an almost continual succession of stolen vehicles, sometimes having multiple cars in their possession at once. One can only speculate on how Dague looked back on his transition from Sunday school teacher to bandit.

Their crime spree reached its height just after Christmas 1929. On Thursday, December 26, Schroeder, Dague, Tom Crawford (Schroeder's brother) and her son arrived in Butler County in a green Chevrolet. They checked into what was the Arlington Hotel and spent the night. The following morning, after forty-five minutes of reconnaissance outside the P.H. Butler grocery store, Schroeder and Dague went into the establishment, leaving Crawford outside to watch the front. Upon entering the store, Schroeder sauntered to the counter to buy fresh apples. While the manager had his back turned to fetch her order, Dague crept behind him and jammed his pistol in his side. When the startled manager turned around, Schroeder also had her pistol unholstered and aimed at his abdomen. As they had done so many times before, the pair bound and gagged the manager in the backroom. While Dague finished subduing the proprietor, Schroeder began to attend to the cash register. Meanwhile, an anxious and curious Crawford, new to this type of lifestyle, abandoned his post and walked into the store.

With no "eyes" on the entrance, an elderly man was able to enter. He was quickly intercepted by the now-exasperated Schroeder and "persuaded" to go to the backroom. Like the manager, he was also bound. Obliging the pleas of the elderly gentleman, Schroeder removed the man's dentures before stuffing a handkerchief in his mouth and gagging him. With the cash register empty, the three quickly rummaged through their captives' pockets, taking their valuables, and then looted the rest of the store, taking a few packs of cigarettes and whatever else suited their fancy. According to eyewitnesses, the three bandits then calmly walked out with their bounty. As they exited, a woman was walking into the establishment. Schroeder kindly told her, "The manager will be out in a minute," and then entered their faded green vehicle. The car pulled away, taking a westerly route on Butler–New Castle Road.

Soon after their departure, the captives were discovered by a local pharmacist and, upon being freed, contacted the Butler authorities. Eyewitnesses who saw the fleeing crooks conveyed to the authorities the make and color of the car, along with the direction they were headed. This information was radioed to all the surrounding police barracks to set up roadblocks on all possible routes out of the county. With Butler on lockdown, one of the only routes available for the crooks to escape was the one they were currently on.

For the troopers in New Castle, the day began like any other day, but the morning routine was broken at 11:40 a.m. with the call from the Butler County Headquarters. First Sergeant Martin J. "Bulldog" Crowley was the one who phoned in to the New Castle police barracks. Two officers responded to the call, Corporal Brady Paul and Private Earnest Moore. Once past the opening formalities, the Butler County sergeant launched into the situation:

> *Corporal Paul, we've just had a holdup here in Butler. We're looking for a short blonde woman, a bit heavy set and wearing all black…and a tall slender fellow with a red mustache. He was wearing a dark overcoat…long overcoat…and there might be another guy with them…we're just not sure yet. Might be driving a sedan. The city police here got men on foot looking and some in autos driving toward Kittanning, but they could just as well be headed toward New Castle. We should get road blocks set up on the Butler–New Castle road. Will you take care of this right away Corporal?*

"I'll get on it right away, Sergeant!" Paul dutifully responded. The New Castle state police headquarters was located across from the train station at the Colonial Hotel on East Washington Street (now a parking lot). With orders to set up a check station, the officers quickly departed from the barracks and headed toward what is now Rosepoint.

Corporal Paul and Private Moore rode in a motorcycle with a sidecar accompaniment—Paul driving and Moore in the sidecar—despite the chilly climate of Pennsylvania's winter. The total trip took roughly twenty minutes, and the officers arrived in Shenango Township around noon. The officers immediately began stopping vehicles heading west on Butler–New Castle Road. Their presence drew the attention of some of the residents in

Corporal Brady Paul, who was brutally shot by Irene Schroeder. *Courtesy of the Lawrence County Historical Society.*

the surrounding community, and according to their testimonies, along with Moore's, one can piece together the events that followed. Upon arriving at their destination, the officers had stopped six cars without incident. At this point, a green four-door Chevrolet coach approached the two-man blockade. Dague was driving, with Schroeder in the passenger seat and Crawford and the child in the back seat. Once the car came to a complete stop, Paul asked to see the driver's identification. Noting the resemblance of this vehicle to the one described in the call, Moore went to the rear of the vehicle to check the license plate. At this point, Moore was alerted to Paul slowly backing up, hands half raised, as Dague and Schroeder advanced with pistols aimed at his chest. Apparently, Dague produced his driver's license and the corporal asked him to take the card out of its holder. Instead, Dague threw the wallet to the side and forced his way out of the driver's side door with Schroeder close behind. Both had their pistols drawn on the surprised trooper, who automatically began walking backward away from the two.

Glenn and Irene

During the subsequent trial, Moore testified that while Paul was backing away, he urged Moore to draw his pistol. Suddenly, shots rang out from the back seat of the vehicle. Crawford wildly unloaded shots through the back window, aimed at Moore. Dague joined in and unloaded a couple shots at Moore. Two bullets found their target, taking a piece of his nose and part of his scalp. Moore found cover around the front of the car and used the radiator as a shield. It was here that he began to fade in and out of consciousness.

Eyewitnesses Eva Baldwin and her sons testified that as Paul continued to back away, Schroeder pulled the trigger of her pistol. She unloaded her weapon at pointblank range on Paul, with four bullets piercing his body. One hit his leg, one hit his arm and two sank into his abdomen. According to the Baldwins and other bystanders, Paul continued to back away during Schroeder's volley until his back hit a nearby utility pole. It was there that he crumpled to the ground. Satisfied, the bandits finally ceased firing and rushed back to their car. Before fleeing, Dague had to attend to the unconscious trooper blocking his exit. He ruthlessly kicked the unresponsive officer until he was cleared from the path of the car. This took only seconds, after which, Dague rushed back to the driver's seat and began to flee. The wounded corporal, with his pistol now freed from its holster, in desperation began to unload rounds into the speeding car until it vanished into the snow-covered countryside.

George Book, a driver for a local bottling company who was driving west on the same road, happened upon the ending of the shootout and corroborated the Baldwins' story. He attested that Schroeder had her gun drawn on the officers. After the shooting, he noted that the couple climbed back into the car and fled westward, toward New Castle. Once clear of the danger, Book rushed to the aid of the wounded officers. He flagged down another passing car and, with their aid, helped Paul into his truck and assisted the conscious but delirious Moore. He quickly drove the mortally wounded Paul back to the Colonial Hotel for help. Though Paul's abdominal wounds were causing him serious amounts of pain, he surprisingly still maintained consciousness and motor faculties. Upon arrival at the barracks, an ambulance was summoned, and Paul was rushed to Jameson Memorial Hospital on Wilmington Avenue on the north side of town.

While Paul was being transported to the hospital, the second car arrived, delivering Private Moore. Moore weakly walked into the hotel and briefly talked to the owners before making his own trip to the hospital. The owners of the Colonial Hotel, John and Mollie Crowl, did not mind housing the troopers in their establishment. Their presence provided them with ensured safety and business. Over the years, the couple grew close to "the boys." As Moore departed to seek medical attention, Mrs. Crowl decided to accompany him. She wanted to see how Paul was doing and at the very least provide comfort.

By this point, Paul was taken in for operation; however, upon examination, the doctors realized there was little they could do to save the wounded trooper. With two bullets lodged inside the abdomen, the available medical resources could not help him. Since he would not survive any operation, all that could be done was to make him as comfortable as possible. Though in much pain, he was still able to communicate with those surrounding him. By this point, Mollie Crowl had arrived at the hospital and made her way to his side. She stated that in the last few minutes of his life he told her, "Tell the boys I did my duty, tell them I did the best I could. You will soon see my mother, because I am dying. Kiss mother goodbye for me." According to the coroner's report, Corporal Brady Clemens Paul was pronounced dead at 12:55 p.m. from internal hemorrhaging. Officer Moore managed to make a full recovery from his minor physical wounds, but the emotional wounds proved to take a much longer recovery time.

As New Castle began to grieve for a fallen officer, the bandits—Schroeder, Dague and Crawford—were scrambling to get away from the city undetected. To achieve this, they needed to quickly abandon their vehicle. Since every officer in the nearby area was on the lookout for them and since their recent entanglement with the law had left a slew of fresh bullet holes decorating the entire rear of the car, their chances of escape were slim at best. The murderers continued west on the Butler–New Castle drag until they spotted a man and woman sitting in a new Chrysler Roadster in a parking lot. They were just about to pull out and head for the city.

For Schroeder and Dague, ditching their conspicuous vehicle was top priority, so they followed their target and forced the Roadster onto the berm of the road. At this point, Dague and Schroeder exited their vehicle with guns drawn. They forced the couple from the Roadster and transferred little Donnie and their possessions from the bullet-ridden Chevy to their newly acquired vehicle. The owner of the now stolen Roadster and a separate witness phoned in to the police to report the incident. In light of the shooting of Corporal Paul, this seemed to be low on the police priority list until the descriptions of the robbers and the abandoned vehicle were relayed. At this point, police swarmed to the scene and immediately impounded and searched the car.

The memorial to Corporal Brady Paul, located near the site of his shooting. *Authors' collection.*

Though they managed to find a new car and were probably very pleased with their success, in their haste, the bandits made two costly mistakes. First, they abandoned a conspicuous vehicle in exchange for another conspicuous vehicle. Second, by leaving the green Chevy behind, important clues were discovered that would lead police back to their hometown of Wheeling, West Virginia. Upon examination, officials discovered that even though the abandoned vehicle bore Ohio license plates, the car was from St. Louis. Apparently, Dague and Schroeder had acquired the vehicle in a similar heist back in Missouri. Moreover, the plates came from another stolen vehicle from Toledo, Ohio. From this, detectives gained significant insight into the lifestyle of their outlaw couple and came to the realization that Dague and Schroeder were hardened criminals. With this epiphany also came the understanding that these two were in it for the long haul and the chances of them turning themselves in were slim.

More important clues that ultimately led officials to the outlaws' hometown came from inside the vehicle. Of these, the most damning was a receipt from a Wheeling department store. With officials now having a hunch on the killers' origin and the make and model of the vehicle they were driving, the anonymity of Schroeder and Dague would soon vanish, and their names and faces would paint the headlines of every major newspaper in the region. This, of course, was still unknown to the killers. As far as they were aware, they had just successfully avoided capture, and as long as they made it home undetected, no one would be able to trace them.

While police scoured the abandoned Chevy, the bandits, accompanied by four-year-old Donnie, were southbound, heading back to hometown Wheeling. The details of their flight out of Pennsylvania become murky due to many versions of this story told by Mrs. Schroeder herself but also because a restaurant owner testified to serving the outlaws dinner along a route that the bandits deny ever taking. According to Beryl Miller, she remembered serving the group dinner around 5:00 p.m. at her restaurant in Monaca. She claimed that the group consisted of two men and one woman, accompanied by a little boy. She further claimed to remember that the group appeared edgy and that the boy was slow in his eating and the woman attempted to hurry him through his meal.

According to Schroeder, the above tale was a fabrication; not only did they not eat at Miller's restaurant but they did not even travel down Route 18. In her telling of the story, she stated that they took Route 108 to Ohio before heading south by way of back roads. It is there that she dropped Donnie off at her father's house in Benwood, West Virginia, after which she and Glenn made the journey back to Wheeling and stayed the night in a garage they rented to house their stolen cars. The following day, the two decided to switch cars and seek asylum in their Parkersburg apartment. Tom Crawford decided to go his own way at some point during the trek to Benwood and was never located by the authorities.

For the next two days, people claimed to have seen the pair around their hometown. The two still did not know that the law was as close as it was to locating them. It was not until December 30 that the media reported the names of Irene Schroeder, Glenn Dague and Thomas Crawford as potential suspects involved in the New Castle police killing of Brady Paul. At this point, Glenn and Irene had already left home and decided on a westward course to avoid capture. As the two went on the lam, detectives and officers began to scour Wheeling and the surrounding area, along with all of their relatives and details of each of their lives.

Through painstaking research and interviews of the bandits' relatives, detectives meticulously pieced together the lives of the murderous duo. Their scouring quickly led them to the house of Ray and Ruby Schroeder, Irene's brother-in-law and sister. When detectives came to interview the pair, they discovered that Donnie was staying there and demanded to question the child alone. The adults protested such an interrogation. Despite the family's unwillingness to let Donnie be questioned, officials still managed to hold the interview, during which the four-year-old gave detectives everything they needed to sign the death warrant for his mother. Among the information that Donnie shared about his mother, the most pertinent was his interpretation of what happened in New Castle. According to the interviewing detectives, Donnie said, "Mama shot a cop, 'jest' like you!" Detectives quickly decided to take the child back to New Castle to be placed in a juvenile detention home. It was the hope of the detectives that this move would draw the bandits back to Pennsylvania. The ploy proved unsuccessful.

With the release of Donnie's unknowing testimony against his mother, the media now had a face to link to the crime. They dubbed Schroeder the "trigger blonde" and began reprinting the story of the New Castle shootout. Readers could not get enough, and newspapers answered their hunger by printing anything and everything about the fleeing crooks. Before a proper picture could be produced, newspapers began drawing sketches of the bandits that bore hardly any resemblance to Schroeder or Dague. Though the Schroeder family publicly attempted to get Donnie back by claiming kidnapping and police harassment, officials would not relent until the bandits turned themselves in. To the disappointment of the New Castle Police Department, and perhaps the Schroeder family as well, Dague and Schroeder did not return.

In fact, they continued westward, making it to St. Louis without incident or knowledge of anything that was going on back home: the police investigation, the "kidnapping" of Donnie or that a nationwide police bulletin was in circulation depicting them and detailing their crime. It read:

> *Attention: Rewards now totaling $3,400 reported offered for the arrest and conviction of the following fugitives who are wanted for the murder December 27, 1929 of State Highway Patrolman Brady Paul near New Castle, Pennsylvania. Glenn Dague, 34, 5'8" or 9", 170 lbs., stocky built, light sandy hair, smooth shaven, small red mustache; Irene Schroeder alias Irene Crawford, 35, 5'2" or 4", 140 lbs., blonde hair light complexion, heavily rouged; Tom Crawford, 25, 5'10", 165–170 lbs.*

To the detriment of the bandits, the police bulletin arrived in St. Louis on the same day they did. When they stopped for information, they learned of the investigation and the manhunt. Armed with this knowledge, they felt it was best to leave such a big city as quickly as possible. On their way out of town, a passing police officer, William Kiessling, saw the pair driving away and noted the resemblance between the two and the depiction supplied by the bulletin. He decided to follow his hunch and stop the pair. Dague, out of fear and frustration, greeted the officer with a gun aimed at his head. Instead of stopping, the trooper rushed the bandit. Dague was startled and, in response, pulled the trigger, shooting Kiessling in the arm. Though shot, the officer continued after his mark and wrapped Dague up with his arm, attempting to bring him to the ground. A scuffle broke out between the two, with Dague landing a well-aimed punch to the officer's face, which briefly incapacitated him. Schroeder and Dague disarmed the dazed and wounded officer and quickly fled the scene, heading south.

The two managed to make it all the way to Arizona, picking up hitchhikers along the way, which proved beneficial because they would send them into stores and gas stations to make their purchases for them. This could account for how they made such a long trip without being detected. Their overall goal was to make it to California, heading south first to throw off the authorities. It was in Arizona, however, that their run would come to a dramatic ending. Now accompanied by hitchhiker and fugitive Joe Wells, the trio pulled into a gas station for a quick meal and to fuel up their car. As the two men were inside, Schroeder was approached by a deputy. When asked for the registration of the vehicle, Schroeder refused. The deputy then attempted to enter the vehicle and drive it back to the nearby station. The two men were on their way back to the vehicle when the deputy entered the car. Dague quickly put an end to the trooper's plan and held him hostage until he showed them how to get back to the interstate. Unknown to the trio, the trooper led them right into a police roadblock where a shootout erupted between the bandits and the officers. Amid the gunfire, the hostage deputy was accidentally shot in the wrist by fellow police officers.

After the close call, the three abandoned their vehicle and, under the cover of night, fled into the nearby Estrada Mountains. The next morning, officers rounded up a posse and followed the fleeing outlaws, trapping them in a cave. Like a true western, a shootout occurred on the hot Arizona desert—outlaws against the law. Of course, the media sensationalized the whole incident. Though shots were fired between both parties, only one person was hit. Schroeder sustained a slight wound from a bullet grazing her neck. Eventually (and anticlimactically), the bandits surrendered to the Arizona police, who immediately identified them as Irene Schroeder and Glenn

Dague from the circulating police bulletin. Though originally thought to be Tom Crawford, Joe Wells's identity was discovered, and he was sent back to federal prison.

Though authorities believed they had the two who supposedly gunned down Officer Brady Paul, the captured crooks denied being involved with any such thing. Moreover, they denied being Schroeder and Dague. Instead, they insisted their names were Albert and Mildred Winthrop and that they were headed west to California to find work. An Arizona official notified the New Castle police that they thought they had captured Schroeder and Dague but would need photo identification sent to be sure. He was quickly obliged and, upon receiving the photos, phoned back that he did indeed believe he had captured the bandits in question. With this confirmation, Governor John S. Fisher signed extradition papers for the pair to be brought back to Pennsylvania.

Dozens of local newspaper reporters, as well as officer Earnest Moore, accompanied the authorities who were charged with extraditing the bandits back to Pennsylvania. They wanted a glimpse of the pair and, if they were lucky, an interview with the "trigger blonde" and her murderous boyfriend. Upon arrival, the group visited the pair in prison and attempted to get a confession or, at the very least, an admission of their true identity. Though both refused to give a confession, Dague did eventually succumb and admit who he was. Schroeder, on the other hand, held out longer, claiming to be Mrs. Winthrop even after Private Moore positively identified her. A slew of tactics were employed to elicit an admission of her identity, including calling Donnie on the phone and having Schroeder talk to him. She threw the receiver back at the detectives and denied having a child.

On Tuesday, January 21, 1930, the outlaw couple was transported back to New Castle to await trial. It took four days, and on arrival, hundreds of people lined the station to see the outlaws who had captured headlines for the past month. To the disappointment of the spectators, officials quickly escorted Glenn and Irene from the train and to the Lawrence County Jail, making for a very anticlimactic show. The outlaws were separated and sent to their designated cells. Now began the wait for the trial to determine their fate. Though they were imprisoned, both enjoyed the benefits of their brief fame. With a constant flow of newspaper reporters and frequent visits from family, the pair had much to fill their time. Both of the outlaws, but especially Schroeder, received packages, gifts and letters from well-wishers.

By mid-February, a jury had been selected to try the case, and a date was set for March 12, 1930. After their identities were confirmed, Schroeder

A partial newspaper clipping from the time of Glenn Dague's trial. The press covered the case in great detail. *Courtesy of the Lawrence County Historical Society.*

and Dague painted a glorious picture of their undying love for each other. "Their passionate love that they had for one another" was devoured by the media and made the front pages of the newspapers. Perhaps the pair hoped that sympathy would be given from the public by taking focus off the crimes and onto their relationship. Whatever the reason for it was, the public could not get enough of their story, and Schroeder and Dague fed their desire with embellished stories of their exploits and the love they shared for each other through it all.

People jammed into the courtroom to hear for themselves what truly transpired on Butler Road. Among them were the family and loved ones of Corporal Brady Paul, who not only desired closure but also justice for the fallen trooper. The pair was tried separately, with Schroeder's trial taking place first. The trial took eleven days, during which spectators were given an in-depth look into the life of Irene Schroeder. During her case, the prosecutor brought in over seventy witnesses to testify. From grocery store clerks to witnesses on Butler Road, the sins of Schroeder were revealed on the witness stand. As an answer to this, Schroeder's defense blamed her deviant ways on her falling on her head as a young child.

During the trial, details about the shooting of Brady Paul were clouded because both Schroeder and Dague claimed to have carried the gun that allegedly delivered the fatal shot. The bullets that were retrieved from the body of the fallen officer were from a .38-caliber pistol. This

Irene Schroeder (center) heading to court. *Courtesy of the Lawrence County Historical Society.*

The Lawrence County Courthouse in the 1920s. Glenn Dague and Irene Schroeder were tried within its walls. *Courtesy of the Lawrence County Historical Society.*

discrepancy was quickly resolved with the testimony of numerous victims who claimed that Schroeder had the bigger gun when they were being robbed. Moreover, the testimony of the Baldwins further confirmed that Schroeder was the shooter.

On March 21, both the prosecution and the defense delivered their closing statements. Defense attorney Thomas Dickey was first to speak. In his statement, he said:

> *We say Private Moore of the Highway Patrol shot Corporal Brady Paul! We say this fearlessly and not caring for whatever effect it may have! If this man were working for me, I wouldn't have him in my presence for fifteen minutes! He is responsible for the death of his fellow officer! He failed to do his duty and cringed and ran for safety when ordered by his superior officer, Paul, to draw his gun and fight! He ran to the front of the car, crouching there shivering, finally drawing his gun to shoot and shoot*

WESTERN STATE PENITENTIARY
OF PENNSYLVANIA

ROCKVIEW, PA.

STANLEY P. ASHE
WARDEN

ELECTROCUTION BUILDING

February 19, 1931.

Commonwealth of Pennsylvania

vs

IRENE SCHROEDER alias IRENE SCHRADER

To_____Frank N. Johnston, Esquire,___High Sheriff

County of_____Lawrence_____and to any Warden, Prison Keeper or

Officer of this Commonwealth having the custody of__Irene Schroeder alias Irene Schrader

GREETING:

By virtue of a warrant issued_____December 10, 1930_____

by____Honorable John S. Fisher,_____Governor of the Commonwealth of Pennsylvania,

commanding me to cause one_____Irene Schroeder alias Irene Schrader_____to be

executed in this institution in the manner prescribed by law, I hereby notify you to forthwith deliver the

said__Irene Schroeder alias Irene Schrader__to the Electrocution Building of the Western State

Penitentiary of Pennsylvania, Rockview, Center County, Pa., where_____she_____shall remain until the

penalty of death has been legally inflicted or until lawfully discharged from my custody.

_____
WARDEN

SEAL

By_____
DEPUTY WARDEN

The document issued by Warden Stanley Ashe of Rockview Penitentiary ordering the transfer of Irene Schroeder to his penitentiary for execution. *Courtesy of the Lawrence County Historical Society.*

*wildly! He does not know what happened to those shots from his gun…
and yet…they had been used!*

This heated accusation of Moore was not taken well by the crowd and
did little to sway the jury's mind. After deliberating for only one hour, it
sentenced Schroeder to death by the electric chair. The defendant surprisingly
showed little emotion to the news of her sentencing. In fact, when her fate
was announced, Schroeder's sisters began to weep aloud. Schroeder turned
quickly to them and angrily yelled, "God-damned-it shut up!"

Dague's trial began on March 24 and only lasted a few days. It ended in
the same manner: Dague was also sentenced to death. For the next eleven
months, the pair awaited the chair in the New Castle prison and tried
desperately to avoid their fate. They made various appeals, all to no avail.
Both then claimed to have never killed Brady Paul and used the defense's
statement that Moore was the one responsible for Paul's death. On February
20, 1931, Schroeder and Dague were transferred to Rockview Penitentiary
in Bellefonte. There they waited for three days. The killers held onto a
distant hope that the governor would call and stop the executions, but he did
not. On February 23, 1931, Irene Schroeder was led to the chair, followed by
Dague. Irene Schroeder was pronounced dead at 7:05 a.m., becoming the
first woman of Pennsylvania to be executed by electric chair. Dague followed
soon after.

After their executions, a letter that Dague wrote and a letter from
Schroeder to her son, Donnie, were made public. In them, they both claim
innocence and maintain that Earnest Moore was the one who killed Brady
Paul. Both explained that they were led astray and were "sinners" but claim
to have found Jesus during their time in prison. In Schroeder's last letter,
she tells Donnie, "My hope and prayer is that you will always be a good
Christian boy and man. When you are tempted to do anything wrong, just
pause a moment and ask God to guide you in the way he would have you
do. May God bless and keep you to meet me at his throne of love and mercy.
From your loving mamma, Irene Schroeder."

ROBBERY ON THE TRACKS

During the height of its industrial era, western Pennsylvania had thousands of miles of railroad tracks and streetcar lines to transport raw materials, finished products and people. Those trains and streetcars also carried money and other valuables, making them a target for daring bandits and gangs. Though frequently portrayed as a common crime in the late 1800s, often occurring in the American West, train robberies actually reached their peak across the United States during the 1920s. Numerous train and streetcar robberies and attempted robberies were reported in western Pennsylvania over the years. Most of the time the bandits would be captured, but occasionally, they escaped the law. This section includes just a few of the many such robberies that plagued this region.

The Erie Railroad Holdup

At 11:00 p.m. on June 30, 1911, Erie railroad officials heard a labored voice through their phone line saying, "We've been robbed! We've been robbed! Maybe lots are shot." The man relaying this urgent news was Conductor H.D. Rooney of the Philadelphia and Erie No. 47 passenger train, which was scheduled to arrive at 10:10 p.m. Just before 10:00 p.m., the train was about five miles from its destination and making good time. As it rounded a large bend, the engineer noticed that a large obstruction made up of railroad ties and telegraph lines was assembled on the track. Immediately, he slammed on the emergency brake and attempted to halt the train before hitting the pile of debris. He managed only to slow it down before crashing into the makeshift barricade.

The passengers onboard first thought that they had collided with another train and began to exit their coaches to have a better look. As the curious began to pour out of the train, gunshots rang out through the night and voices demanded the passengers return to their seats. By now, the passengers began to deduce that this was no accidental collision and that this was a robbery of some sort. For the bandits, this was a well-thought-out heist. The location was ideal for this type of crime, with one side of the track being dense forest and the other a three-hundred-foot ravine. Once the train fully stopped, the masked robbers emerged from their hiding places and began to direct the passengers back to their seats. When some of the passengers panicked and attempted to flee, a few well-aimed shots were fired down the sides of the train cars to persuade them to return to their seats. Though most passengers were contained inside the cars, there was still confusion and panic, and a number of women fainted.

A few brave passengers attempted to fight back. In one case, a man managed to grab hold of one of the robbers and attempted to grapple him to the ground. The enraged bandit fought back and mercilessly picked up the passenger and threw him over the embankment and down into the ravine. The passenger received serious injuries but would be recovered and transported to the hospital.

Once the passengers were under control, the bandits headed inside toward the mail car that held the train's loot. A gun battle ensued between train officials and the desperados. C.H. Block, the Erie mail clerk, unloaded two revolvers at the masked bandits before he was struck in the thigh by a bullet. Three other train officials were wounded: an express man was shot through the left leg, and the brakeman sustained a flesh wound. Conductor Rooney was also injured while he unloaded a revolver he borrowed from a passenger. It is possible that Rooney wounded one of the robbers. While he attempted to defend his train, however, one of the robbers picked up a large stone and bludgeoned the conductor in the back. With all hostility subdued, the robbers grabbed sacks of mail and quickly fled the scene.

Up until the time that the call was received, Erie train officials were becoming increasingly anxious as the train's tardiness stretched into an hour. They received a telegraph from Belle Valley just before the robbery had occurred that the train had passed and was on time. Back on the tracks, the severely wounded Rooney abandoned the train and crawled through the woods to a local farmhouse, where he made the call to the Erie headquarters confirming their fears.

Within thirty minutes of this call, word of the holdup spread like wildfire through the city of Erie, and a crowd of five thousand began to assemble at the station for the No. 47's late arrival, anticipating the worst. Upon arrival, two coaches were filled with detectives and officials and rushed back to the scene of the holdup. Immediately, railroad detectives began scouring the tracks with lanterns dotting the landscape. While searching the scene, detectives discovered fused dynamite wrapped in a Polish newspaper under a tree stump. It appeared to be the robbers' back-up plan if the obstruction did not work. Bloodstains and footprints led officials down to the bottom of the ravine, where they believed the injured robber washed and dressed his wounds.

During the next couple of days, rumors flew that the robbers were foreigners, and a few locals claimed to have seen foreigners walking the tracks every evening, including the evening of the robbery. Mrs. F.J. Aman claimed that she saw a foreigner the morning following the train robbery limping past her home. It turned out not to be the case. Investigations lasted until July 7, when eight men were arrested for the holdup: Joseph Moran, Charles Fried, Matt Cummings, Henry Fried, Frank King, Frank Ryan, James Martin and Thomas Harrington. These men were also wanted for the killing of an Erie police officer from the previous year.

THE BELSANO TRAIN ROBBERY

On the morning of October 11, 1924, Warren "Bucky" Mentch, an engineer on the Cambria and Indiana Railroad, was making a normal run heading to the Ebensburg Coal Company at Colver in Cambria County. Among his passengers were two guards, Joseph Davis and James Garman, who were watching over the coal company payroll, which totaled over $33,000. At about 9:00 a.m., Mentch, who was running a little late, was attempting to make up time on the portion of the run that passed through the town of Belsano. It had a small station that was tied into a concrete bridge, now PA Route 271, and the tracks crossed only a few feet away. According to Mentch, "There was a little 2x4 station there, and when someone was standing there you could be sure he wanted to board the train; there wasn't much else there." This was a rarity, so when the brakeman alerted him to the presence of a man waiting at the Concrete Bridge, Mentch had to slam on the emergency brake to get it stopped in time.

Upon stopping, he leaned out the cab window to speak. Before he could talk, a shot broke the morning silence, and a bullet flew right above his head and became embedded in the top of the cab. At the same time, bandits appeared out of the brush and directed the crew off the train and lined them against the engine. Concerned for the train and their well-being, Mentch asked if he could turn off the engine's injector to prevent a potential explosion. The bandits, oblivious to the danger, quickly told him no, saying, "What's the difference, it don't belong to us." According to Mentch, he couldn't hear what was going on inside the train due to the noise from the engine.

Unknown to the crew, the heist had begun before the train even stopped at Belsano. As soon as the train began to brake at the Concrete Bridge intersection, two passengers already onboard made their way to the rear of the compartment and drew guns. Without hesitation, they shot Garman, who died shortly after, and disarmed the shocked Davis. When the train stopped, the bandits onboard were joined by the others and efficiently removed the safe. The robbers threw the safe from the train car, carried/dragged it to a parked automobile nearby and fled the scene.

The shaken crew quickly boarded the train and made their way to Colver, where they took the corpse of Garman to the hospital and reported the robbery to the state police. According to local papers, a posse of over one hundred men was sent to the scene and canvassed the surrounding area. Roadblocks were also set up all over the region, but to no avail. Circulars were sent to other states describing the thieves, and a reward for $1,000 was offered for information leading to their arrest.

Within two weeks of the circulars being sent, two men were arrested in Indiana. Mechleo Bassi and Anthony Pezzi were in possession of $3,000 and a handgun when they were caught. They were found guilty of first-degree murder, and on February 23, 1925, both were executed by electric chair. Though two men were brought to justice for the death of James Garman and the robbery of over $33,000, the rest of the gang and the money were never found. The location of the stolen money still remains a mystery. Some believe that the money was buried in Belsano near the Concrete Bridge.

ROBBERY ON THE STREETCAR

On a warm Saturday evening in late May 1908, a West Penn streetcar embarked on its usual run from the city of McKeesport to the town of Elizabeth. It was an open summer car, which allowed its passengers to experience the pleasant late spring air. Everything was proceeding as usual until the streetcar passed through the town of Boston. It was there that two men signaled to board the car at Smithfield Street as it approached on the tracks. When it slowed, one man jumped on the front platform and the other jumped onto the rear platform. The men seemed to be acting unusual, and each wore a handkerchief around his neck like a western outlaw. As the streetcar moved toward Shaner's Corner, the man on the front platform pulled a gun and pointed it at the motorman, Jesse Reed. He demanded that the startled motorman bring the car to a halt and turn over his valuables. Reed complied, but instead of handing his wallet directly to the bandit, he threw it away from himself and the assailant. The robber became angry and threatened to kill Reed if he attempted to move or make any noise while he recovered the wallet. The outlaw was in luck, because Reed had been paid the day before.

When the car began to slow, the man on the rear platform made his move. He, too, pulled a revolver and used it to relieve the conductor, Rueben Prescott, of his watch and wallet. When they were finished with the motorman and conductor, the two bandits stepped into the main car. The one in the front demanded to know if any of the eleven passengers had weapons. They all replied that they did not. Within minutes, the pair of robbers took all of the passengers' valuables and money. As they were stepping out of the car to make their escape, one of the men fired two shots into the air as a warning, attempting to dissuade anyone from coming after them or alerting authorities before they escaped. The bandits darted toward the woods, which were not far from the track. Waiting in the trees were two horses that they had stolen earlier from Wiley's Livery in nearby Elizabeth.

Only hours after leaving the scene of the streetcar robbery, the bandits struck again on a dark road in Elizabeth. Local farmer John Mowry and his wife were riding in their buggy when the two bandits stepped onto the road in front of them with guns drawn and handkerchiefs pulled over their faces. One robber seized the reins to the horses while the other ordered Mowry out of the buggy. When he hesitated, the outlaw pressed the barrel of the gun against his head and dragged him out by his coat. Mrs. Mowry was also ordered out, and she complied. The robbers took all the money that Mowry was carrying—fifteen dollars—but did not notice Mrs. Mowry's jewelry. The farmer and his wife were then ordered back into the buggy and were told to ride away quietly.

In the meantime, local authorities, led by Allegheny County detective John Englert, began their investigation. Englert gathered some solid leads and was able to track the horses used in the getaway because one was missing a shoe. While he verified his evidence and confirmed the identity of the robbers, he told the local press that he had no leads and that there was little chance the bandits would be caught. It was part of his strategy to make sure the bandits kept their guard down. Meanwhile, he assembled a posse to apprehend the bandits at an old home on Bellebridge Hill that they used as a hideout.

On June 6, Detective Englert and Constable Jones approached the house before additional backup had arrived. As they approached, the door suddenly flew open and one of the bandits, later identified as Thomas Manning, emerged firing a gun in each hand. One of the shots hit Englert's right arm, but that did not prevent him from firing back. The detective carefully aimed and fired five shots into Manning, who stumbled back into the house and collapsed on the floor. Englert and Jones both took cover and called for more officers. A car full of detectives sped to the scene and within minutes had the house surrounded. The second bandit, John Patterson, was hiding inside with his wife, child and younger brother. After seeing the condition of his partner, he decided to surrender without a fight. Manning was transported to McKeesport Hospital but died later that day from the wounds he received. Police were able to recover some of the items stolen during the streetcar holdup, as well as evidence to link the pair to several other local robberies.

THE BIDDLE BOYS ESCAPE

At the turn of the twentieth century, many Pittsburgh residents and businesses became victims of the violent Chloroform Gang. Their ominous name was derived from their method of subduing their victims: smothering them with rags soaked in ether or chloroform until unconscious. Once their prey was rendered incapacitated, the bandits would loot their surroundings, taking anything of value. This tactic proved to be very successful and was a relatively safe way to rob victims, providing the gang members with a lucrative flow of cash. This band of thieves was led by a pair of brothers—Jack Biddle, age twenty-eight, and Ed Biddle, age twenty-four—who had relocated to the Pittsburgh area from Canada.

On April 12, 1901, the Biddle brothers rounded up their accomplices and made their way to Mount Washington. Their destination was a small but successful grocery store and home owned by Thomas Kahney. After breaking into the building, the gang fell upon the elderly Kahney. The old man struggled with the intruders while they attempted to asphyxiate him. During the fight, one of the bandits who was carrying a gun accidentally discharged his weapon. The shot struck the grocer in the head, killing him instantly. With the robbery turning into a murder, the gang was quick to leave before the police were called.

When the police arrived, fronted by Lieutenant Charles "Buck" McGovern, they quickly scoured the scene for clues. They also utilized their network of paid informants to gain information. By the next day, the lieutenant had the names of the supposed leaders of the "Chloroform Gang" and the address

A map of the Pittsburgh area in 1903. *Authors' collection.*

of where they and a few other bandits were hiding: a house on Fulton Street in Manchester, near the North Shore. Unsure if the informants had accurate information regarding the suspects or their location, McGovern decided to move in anyway. The lieutenant was determined to see the victims of the Chloroform Gang have justice, especially Kahney's family. McGovern quickly amassed a team of officers and headed to the Biddles' suspected hideout. Instead of executing a covert operation, the lieutenant had his officers surround the house, cutting off all potential escape routes.

Inside the house were the Biddle brothers and one of their accomplices, Walter Dorman. Due to the troopers' loud display while getting into positions, the three bandits immediately became aware of what was happening outside. Though initially taken by surprise, the outlaws were quick to assess the situation in which they found themselves. With too many police officers present to make an escape, the bandits were left with two options: make a stand or go quietly. As officers surrounded the house, the three inside prepared for a fight, choosing a darkened room to make their stand.

Back outside, with all exits covered, a small team led by McGovern and his partner, Detective Patrick Fitzgerald, entered and began moving through the house. The Biddles and Dorman waited in the shadows for their moment to release a rain of bullets on the unaware officers. Their wait was short; as soon as detectives entered their room, the gang unloaded on the advancing detectives. The surprised officers were quick to fire back. As bullets wildly flew throughout the room, one found its mark, killing Detective Fitzgerald on the spot. As more and more officers entered the room, the bandits changed their minds and decided that the odds were against them. They would rather take their chances in court. The three surrendered, ending the short-lived shootout. A conflicting account, however, was reported in a local paper claiming that it was solely Ed Biddle who shot down Detective Fitzgerald and that the shootout occurred when the detective entered Ed Biddle's room. However it happened, the trio was taken into custody and put on trial for the murder of the Mount Washington grocer.

During the court proceedings, Walter Dorman testified against the brothers and was rewarded with a life sentence. Betrayed by one of their own, the brothers did not fare as well and were sentenced to hang. Both were put on death row in adjacent cells inside the Allegheny County Jail to await their date of execution. They attempted a series of appeals, all of which were rejected. With all hope exhausted, they placed a formal request to Pennsylvania governor Stone asking to be hanged on separate days. They were adverse to the idea of dying next to each other at the same time and on the same scaffold. Placed in what seemed like an impossible situation, the brothers attempted to have some sort of control over their death.

As they waited for the governor's reply and their date of execution, the brothers sought any sort of comfort. Surprisingly, this comfort came from the most unlikely places. Throughout their trial and subsequent incarceration, the brothers gained quite a bit of attention. The public remembered the slew of robberies committed by the Chloroform Gang. With the added publicity from the Mount Washington murder and the shooting of the detective, the Biddle boys were a household name in the Pittsburgh area. With faces to go along with these heinous crimes, one would think that the public would be revolted by the pair. Shockingly though, many—mostly women—were enamored with the bandit brothers, not for their crimes but their looks. The Biddle brothers were very handsome, and local women swooned over the outlaw pair.

These good looks and fame quickly drew the attention of Warden Peter Soffel's wife, Katherine Soffel. Since the warden's duties occupied much of his time, the Soffel family residence was connected to the jail. Though the warden's life was localized in the same building, much of his time was devoted to his career rather than his wife and children. With her husband constantly preoccupied, Mrs. Soffel would frequent the jail to occupy her time as well. She would use her time to form relationships with the inmates with hopes of rehabilitation. Though against protocol, with her husband and father both working at the jail, this was overlooked. It did not take long before the lure of the famed Biddles led her to their cells. Not only were they endowed with good looks, as the papers depicted, but they were also extremely charming.

In stark contrast to Ed Biddle's looks, Kate Soffel was quite homely. A contemporary description claims that she had a "hook nose, buck teeth, and a hunchback." Mrs. Soffel became particularly fond of the younger brother, Ed Biddle, and began to bring him food and reading material so he could pass the time. Unsure if this was a normal occurrence between Soffel and inmates, the fortunate brother accepted these gifts without complaint. Under different circumstances, Edward would not have looked twice at this plain woman who bore him gifts and visited him regularly. Inside prison, however, Mrs. Soffel had his undivided attention, and she reveled in it. Every visit with the convict deepened her attraction to him.

It was not long before it became apparent to the brothers that the treatment that Ed was receiving was out of the norm. They speculated on the possible motives of the warden's wife and realized that Mrs. Soffel was taken with Edward. With this epiphany, a small spark of hope began to burn within the brothers. If Edward played his cards right, he might be able to not only save himself from the gallows but his brother as well. With the possibility of escape in mind, Edward made courting Mrs. Soffel his top priority. He used any means possible to seduce her, from divulging intimate secrets and fears to writing bad poetry. One of his poems still exists and shows the "depth" of the bandit's creativity:

> *Just a little violet*
> *From across the way*
> *Came to cheer a prisoner*
> *In his cell one day*

As he had hoped, Kate was deeply moved by the bandit's "sensitivity," and his plan of seduction was quick to bear fruit. With every secret that Ed Biddle divulged and with every small moment of intimacy spent with the enthralled Mrs. Soffel, Ed found himself more in control. As she became absorbed with her forbidden lover, her duties as a mother and wife were left unattended, placing a severe strain on her union with her husband. With her marriage practically in ruins, Biddle supplied her with a never-ending flow of compliments and attention, something that was practically devoid in her home. When Edward felt that the "Queen of the Jail" was firmly in the palm of his hand, he was ready to lay plans for an escape. The success of the plan relied heavily on Soffel's devotion to him, which was catalyzed by the rapidly deteriorating state of her marriage. Unknown to her, the warden had already filed for divorce and was spending even less time with his soon-to-be ex-wife.

By December 1901, the Biddles delicately presented Soffel with a vague outline of their plan for escape. It did take not much to sway her; after all, how could she let her "true love" be executed? The most difficult part of the escape would be the cells themselves. Without a key to unlock their doors, the heavy iron bars would prove to be a near-impossible feat. The brothers noted this difficulty and devised a plan to overcome such an obstacle. What they needed was the right set of tools to spring them from their cells, and they convinced Soffel to sneak them in, along with added materials for their high-risk breakout. Utilizing the Holy Bible, Soffel managed to smuggle saw blades in between the pages, as well as wax and chewing gum. She even managed to slip revolvers past the unsuspecting guards.

The Biddles were quick with their work, and by mid-January 1902, the pair had already finished the necessary tasks for escape. Unknown to the guards or warden, they were able to saw through the jail bars, creating a hole just large enough for them to get through and reattaching them with the wax and bubble gum. With their jail cells prepped for escape, the brothers bided their time, waiting for the right opportunity to make their move.

Their date of escape depended heavily on Soffel. Edward conferred with Kate through letters to see when they should plan their escape. Even at this point, Soffel did not yet know what she was going to do—leave with the Biddles or stay in an unhappy relationship that seemed destined to fail. Ed, aware of her indecisiveness, wrote to her, urging her to tell him what she was planning. Their initial plan was for Kate to head for Canada before the brothers escaped and rendezvous at a planned location. Another option posed by the bandit was for her to stay at home and leave her husband a month or so after so as not to arouse suspicion. Biddle himself told her that he thought it would be much easier for them to escape and less suspicious if she would stay at home rather than depart beforehand or with them. In his correspondence, he told her that if she chose this option, then she should go to the Homestead Post Office on March 1 and to collect the mail of Mrs. Charles W. McDonald. Within the mail, she would be provided with information as to their whereabouts. Edward had provided the love-struck Mrs. Soffel with several options. She still made no decision.

Edward did not relent. Even the week before their planned escape, he was insistent on knowing what she planned. In his letter, he stated, "Now, if you go Monday let me know as early as you can. Come close to the window and say 'I will go.' If you decide to stay at home, tell me. Then you will give me permission to go. Everything has been ready since Friday." According to him, whatever her decision was, he was going to escape with his brother that week and warned her not to betray his trust. Before closing his letter, he offered her this warning: "And now, should you take it into your head to do me wrong. Thinking that I would not know it you would make a sad mistake. If you were to let me go ahead and then get me caught I would kill every keeper in the place and then myself next. I'll tell you I'm not to be betrayed."

With that letter, the brothers set on a date, and on the morning of January 30, 1902, the brothers made their move. Around four o'clock in the morning, Mrs. Soffel, taking a leaf from her bandit lover, crept through the dark to where her husband slept and smothered him with chloroform. With the warden incapacitated, the brothers had only to worry about the three guards who had the night shift. The older brother initiated the escape around the same time Kate was chloroforming her husband. Jack urgently called for the guards; his brother was "deathly ill" and in need of medical treatment.

Answering the call, James McGeary rushed to the second floor to where the Biddles were kept and assessed the situation. He was quick to determine that the bandit brother was in dire need of medicine and fetched it at once. Upon his return, he reached through the bars and attempted to hand the agonized Biddle medicine. All the while, Jack stealthily removed his pre-cut jail bars and attacked the unsuspecting guard from behind. The brother managed to wrestle the startled McGeary to the nearby railing, ending the short struggle by tossing the prison guard over the edge, plummeting him to the stone floor more than sixteen feet below.

The younger Biddle was quick to his brother's side, and with revolvers drawn, they hastened to the first floor, where they were met by the second guard. Rather than engaging in more hand-to-hand combat, they deterred the guard's advance by wounding him with their .32-caliber revolvers. This, of course, drew the attention of the third guard, who was on the upper floor. The brothers persuaded him down to the first floor at gunpoint, confiscated the prison keys and locked the three guards in the lower dungeon. With the perimeter clear of pesky prison staff, the brothers, now joined by Mrs. Soffel, visited the guards' dressing room and traded their conspicuous prison garb for suits and ties. With the three guards locked away and the warden chloroformed, the bandits walked through the Soffel residence and out the front door, unlocked the front gate and walked onto Ross Street. With the inmates now free, Mrs. Soffel, in fear of never seeing Ed Biddle again, finally made the decision Biddle had asked of her in his letter. Leaving her husband, four children and home, she decided to join the brothers on their exodus out of Pittsburgh. The trio had little to worry of pursuit for at least a couple hours, until the daylight guards would relieve the night shift at 6:00 a.m. After leaving the jail, they sought refuge and ended up finding it at a boardinghouse in the city, staying there all of Thursday.

Meanwhile, back at the Allegheny County Jail, the daylight shift was quick to discover the missing guards. In their search for the night shift, they discovered the vacant cells, as well as the shamed guards locked in the basement. The alarms were sounded, rousing the still-groggy warden, and police sent to follow any leads. Officials alerted nearby towns of the escaped outlaws. In their thorough search of the prison, officials and prison personnel noticed that Mrs. Soffel also was missing and were quick to make the link between Soffel and the escape. To the embarrassment of the warden, the media latched on to such a scandalous event, and every paper in town was eager to print such a story.

Needless to say, word of the escaped brothers rapidly spread. Soon enough, the owners of the boardinghouse read the newspaper articles detailing the prison break earlier that morning and recognized their guests to be the Biddles with Soffel in tow. As the owners of the boardinghouse excitedly read through the articles, they may have been enticed to turn the bandits in to authorities, especially since a cash reward of $5,000 was offered by the county commissioner's office. Rather than go through the trouble, the owners were content with blackmailing the outlaws by demanding a large sum of money. If they did not pay, they would unfortunately have to turn them in. The Biddles reluctantly complied with the homeowners' demand and paid them handsomely for their refuge. Though blackmailed, the brothers felt relatively safe at this point and were willing to hide out in the home for an indefinite time, at least until the city cooled down. Soffel, on the other hand, began having bad feelings about the place and the people who took them in and thought that they would be caught. For the rest of the day, Soffel aired her feelings, pleading to leave at once; eventually, Ed Biddle conceded. Jack profusely disagreed with this decision and attempted to change his brother's decision, but to no avail.

As soon as it was dark enough to travel safely, Ed and Kate made plans to leave the house and head north. Unwilling to be parted from his brother,

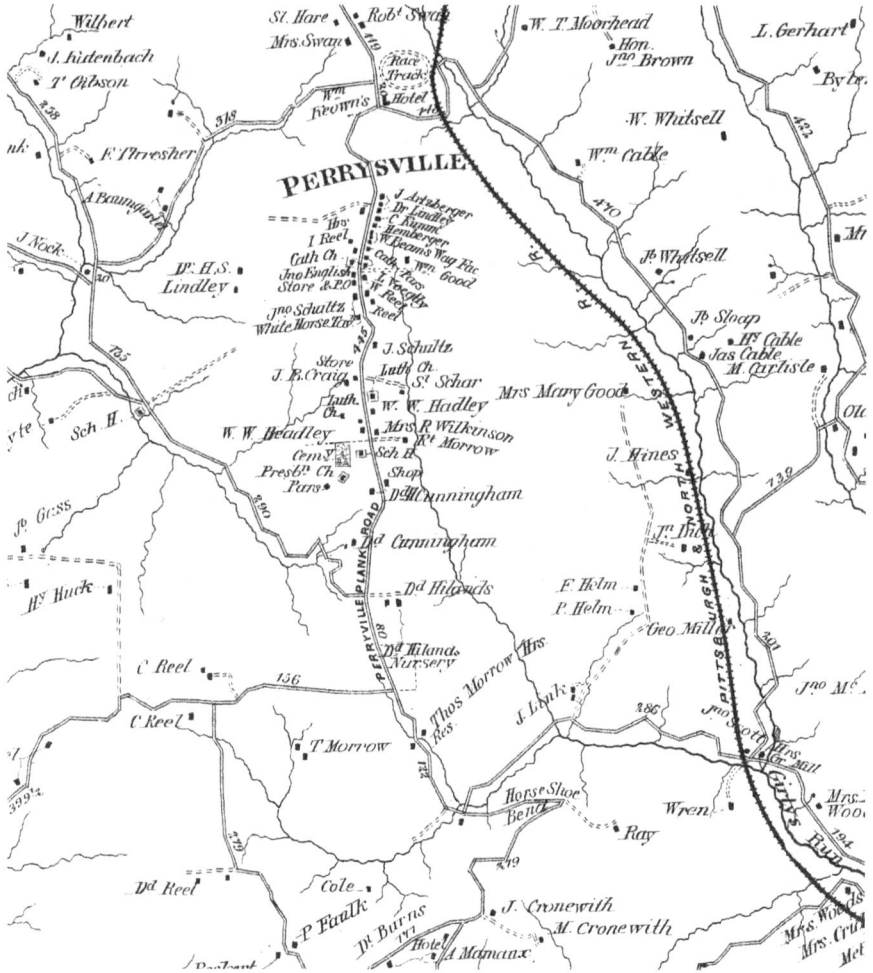

A map of the Perrysville area from the 1876 *Centennial Atlas of Allegheny County. Courtesy of the Library and Archives Division, Senator John Heinz Pittsburgh Regional History Center.*

Jack begrudgingly followed the pair. Bidding their new acquaintances farewell, the fleeing bandits stole through the darkened streets of Pittsburgh until reaching one of the many trolley stations in the city. Deciding to take a northerly course, they boarded a Perrysville Avenue trolley, riding it to the line's end in West View. With no other option, the trio had to proceed on foot through the snow. By Friday evening, they had made it as far north as the village of Perrysville in Ross Township. Seeking shelter from the elements, the three decided to lay low and hide out in a local schoolhouse. The Biddles

The Biddle Boys Escape

The White House Inn in Perrysville, where the Biddle brothers and Mrs. Soffel stopped for food as they fled north. *Courtesy of John Schalcosky of the Ross Township Historical Society.*

knew that they needed to find an alternative mode of travel, and soon. They could only elude capture and, if nothing else, survive the elements for so long. As fortune would have it, not long after leaving the schoolhouse, they happened upon a local farm whose barn was open and managed to steal a horse and sleigh, as well as a shotgun. Before making it out of the village, they needed food and drink and stopped at the White House Inn, an establishment run by Christopher R. Weller. It was the night of January 30, and Weller was tending the bar and entertaining guests. Conflicting accounts arise to who actually went into the inn. One version claims that both Soffel and the brothers came in seeking sustenance; however, the official record maintains that only Edward Biddle entered the establishment. Due to the late hour, Weller did not have any dinner on hand and could only furnish six ham sandwiches. The bandit bought them, along with a pint of whiskey. According to Weller's account, all of the food was unable to fit in the patron's coat pocket, forcing the bandit to remove his revolver to make room. The three did not tarry and were eager to put as many miles between them and the city as possible. Though quick to leave the inn, the frequent stops, coupled with the slow travel by foot, made it well after 1:00 a.m. before the trio was heading north in its stolen sleigh.

As the bandits trotted up snowy Route 19 (Perry Highway), officials were still scouring the city looking for leads when a tip was called in from Perrysville. Apparently, someone found the escaped trio suspicious and

Perry Highway in 1902. Some of the tracks in the road were made by the sleigh stolen by the Biddle brothers and Mrs. Soffel. *Courtesy of John Schalcosky of the Ross Township Historical Society.*

thought that they could potentially be the escapees, so they alerted the police. A posse was quickly amassed by Lieutenant McGovern and headed north. Before departing, city officials wired Butler County police to make them aware of the potential situation. The bandits, unaware of the pursuit, continued along their route until about seven o'clock in the morning. They had made it roughly forty miles north of the city and decided to stop again for food. They located another inn, this one in Cooperstown, and stopped for a hot breakfast. They probably would have made it farther, but Soffel needed to make frequent stops and seek shelter from the cold. The brothers reluctantly obliged, which ultimately hindered their progress.

The Biddle Boys Escape

After breakfast, the outlaws decided to travel west toward Butler. They traveled at a slower pace through the day and only cleared Mount Chestnut by five o'clock that evening. After a detour around the small town, they stopped again for dinner at the residence of J.J. Stephens. After they finished, they continued westward toward Butler, which was only five miles away. Unknown to the bandits, the authorities, who rode at a heavy pace throughout the day, were only a couple miles behind them. In haste to overtake the bandits, the posse, following the tracks of the fleeing trio, made a wrong turn and went eight miles in the wrong direction. Upon discovering their error, they quickly wired to Mount Chestnut for a fresh supply of horses, as well as the Butler police, who by now were also after the bandits. Pittsburgh officers arrived in Mount Chestnut only half an hour after the bandits departed.

With fresh horses awaiting them, the officers changed out the tired steeds and continued after the Biddles and Soffel. With authorities close on their tails and with more horses, men and firepower, the Biddles stood no hope of outracing the law. The Biddles became aware of the pursuers, and instead of continuing west, decided to turn around, heading directly toward the officers. The chase reached its climax at a farm two miles east of Prospect when the bandits were spotted by the police. Conflicting accounts arise to what happened next; one account claims that Lieutenant McGovern hollered out for the bandits to surrender but was greeted with swift gunfire, whereas another account claims that deputies fired on the bandits first. Whatever the case is, these facts are true: the bandits and officers were roughly sixty yards apart before gunfire was exchanged. The Biddles were armed with revolvers and a shotgun, and the deputies were armed with Winchester rifles and high-caliber pistols.

When the shooting broke out, Ed was steering the sleigh, with the other two on the rear. Handing Soffel the reins and warning her to keep down, he and Jack began to unload lead at the deputies. The deputies were quick to respond with gunfire of their own. With superior firepower and training, the officials were deadly accurate, shooting Jack twelve times and Ed twice. The authorities, on the other hand, did not incur a single casualty. The brothers, unable to stand after such a volley, tumbled off the still-moving sleigh onto each other in the snow. With all chances of escape lost, the pair turned their guns on themselves. The older of the two, placing the revolver in his mouth, pulled the trigger twice, whereas Edward decided to shoot himself above his heart; neither was successful in their suicide attempts. Realizing her imminent capture and following the Biddles' lead, Soffel, who was still in the sleigh, also decided to choose death over capture. Grabbing a revolver, Soffel turned it on herself, aimed it at her heart and pulled the trigger. Instead of killing her, the bullet reflected off her corset, thwarting her suicide attempt.

Officers cautiously approached the sprawled-out Biddles. Believing that the brothers were using this as a ploy to lure the officers in close, McGovern ordered his detectives to stay away. One of the detectives, claiming to see Ed Biddle rummage in his coat as if for a pistol, fired another shot into the already wounded bandit. At this point, McGovern himself ran up within five feet of the helpless Biddles and unloaded the rest of his rifle magazine at the two. It was at this point that the Biddles, surprisingly still breathing, meekly surrendered. In the end, Jack was shot by the troopers fifteen times and sustained two wounds by his own hand; Ed was shot twice by the officers and once by himself. Unwilling to take any chances with the slippery pair, detectives shackled the legs and hands of the dying brothers and, along with Soffel, escorted them to the city of Butler. The Biddles headed to jail and Soffel to the hospital.

After the Biddles were imprisoned in the Butler County Jail, hostility arose between the Pittsburgh officers and the Butler County troopers. With the Biddles in the custody of Butler County officials, debate about the $5,000 reward money ensued. This conflict culminated when McGovern and his men attempted to enter the Butler Jail. The entrance was guarded by the Butler troopers, who were armed and refused the Pittsburghers admittance. McGovern and his men, who were positively enraged, drew their weapons, illustrating the extent to which they would go. With McGovern's lead, the Pittsburgh detectives stormed into the jail, luckily without violence. Both parties filed formal charges against the other, but they were later dropped. Once both sides cooled off, the reward money was split evenly among all the officers. However, the media followed and publicized the quarrel and the settlement in the daily paper.

The Biddles, who both lay bleeding in separate cells, were unable to escape death for a second time. Jack, riddled with bullet holes, was quite talkative to those surrounding his cell. He shared with them details of their escape from their prison cells and their flight north. When he began to feel the heaviness of death ease over him, he repented his crimes and claimed his innocence of the shootings of Detective Fitzgerald and the Mount Washington grocer. In his confession he stated:

I know that my time here is short, and you can say for me that I am Christian, and will die a sincere believer in God, and I hope I will have strength enough to say so at the last. I know I have taken part in many wrongdoings, but I have never killed any man, and was never implicated with anyone who did. I wish I could see Mrs. Kahney. I would tell her the truth about the killing of her husband. This life has been tough to me, and the end cannot come too quick, and I don't care how.

His brother, in an adjoining cell, faded in and out of consciousness the last few hours of his life. Before he died, he also managed to choke out a last confession, which strongly mirrored his older brother's sentiments. In his confession, he stated:

I have been accused of a great many serious crimes. I want to say now that I did not kill Detective Fitzgerald, nor did I shoot Thomas Kahney, nor was my brother implicated in the latter affair. Mrs. Soffel aided us in getting out of the county jail. And had it not been for her we would have made our escape to-day. She gave up everything for us. And I was bound to back her. I did not shoot her. She shot herself. I am grateful to the woman who helped us to escape she did it out of sympathy and I persuaded her to do it.

A priest was brought to their cells, and the brothers received last rites. Jack was the first to pass; Ed followed soon after. Immediately, their corpses were sent back to Pittsburgh to be examined and prepared for burial. Upon arrival, the triumphant troopers were met by a mob of people who observed the procession to the morgue. Rather than a celebratory event, many of the people mourned the death of the brothers. To many, the bandit brothers were something of heroes who were trying to escape the long arm of the law.

The corpses were examined by the coroner, and the autopsy revealed that Edward died from the shot he fired into his chest and Jack died from the wounds sustained by the officers; the shots he fired in his mouth did little to contribute to his death. The next day, after the autopsy, the bodies were put on display for three hours by an undertaker on the South Side. This occasion was observed by more than four thousand people, most of whom were women who wished to pay their respects to the handsome outlaws. Many brought flowers and other things to be placed near the bodies. The police and morgue did not anticipate the number of people who showed up, and at one point, the place became so crowded that it became difficult to move. To oblige the pleas of the owners and to prevent potential trouble, the police decided to close the doors to the viewing early. Many spectators were

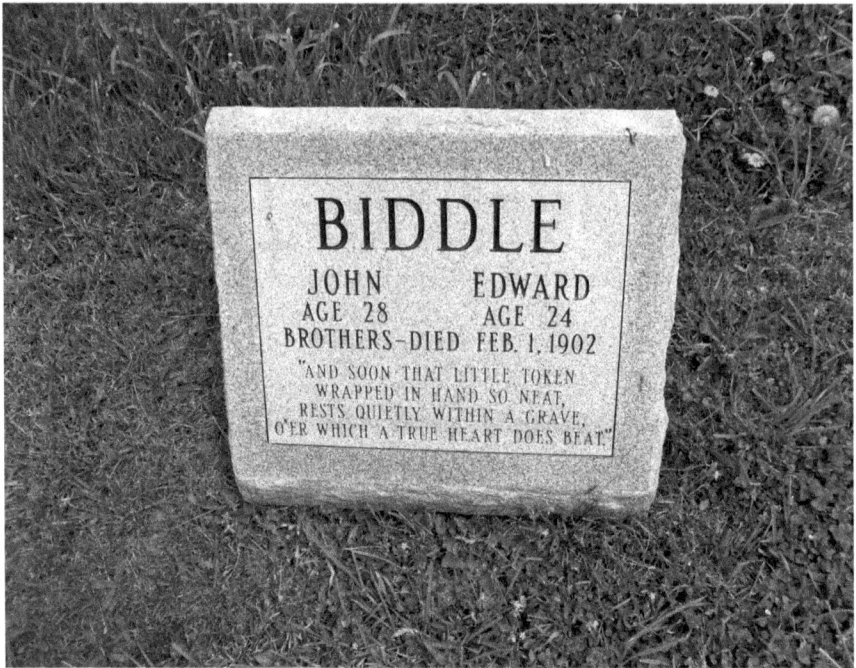

The headstone marking the grave of the Biddle brothers. Originally, the grave was unmarked because they were buried in the poor section of Calvary Cemetery in Pittsburgh. While writing the screenplay for the movie *Mrs. Soffel* for MGM, Ron Nyswance identified the grave and paid for the marker. *Courtesy of Elizabeth Williams.*

displeased with this decision and lingered about the establishment in case the police relented. When this did not happen, many left their flowers on the step or with the undertaker to be placed on their graves.

This type of reception confounded many, especially the officers who had chased down the bandits. How could so much sympathy be elicited for murderers and thieves? A large number of the mourners who made an appearance at the Biddle brothers' viewing believed them to be innocent. This sentiment was reaffirmed when the Biddles' deathbed confessions and claims of innocence were published in the papers. Another factor that contributed to the enormous amount of sympathy for the brothers was the treatment of the bandits when recaptured. These sentiments are illustrated by B.M., a concerned citizen who felt compelled to write to the *New York Times*, calling the capture unnecessary and commenting that the "clubbing and shooting of one of them after they were lying wounded and helpless face down on the snow" was "cowardly and brutal." These reasons, coupled with the publicized quarreling over the prize money between the two posses, contributed to the negative feelings aimed at the officers.

After the autopsy and viewing, the brothers' bodies were handed over to family members, who scheduled their burial for the following Wednesday. Anticipating a large crowd, the city sent troopers to maintain order during the funeral; however, only a small collection of people showed up for their burial—no more than twenty-five—rendering the officials useless. The brothers were given a quiet Roman Catholic burial and were laid to rest in a single grave in Calvary Cemetery.

With the Biddles at peace, Mrs. Soffel, who by now was on the mend from her wounds, had to face the public and her family alone. Once healthy enough to travel, she was transported back to Pittsburgh and indicted for aiding in the escape of the Biddle brothers. Rather than fight, she made a full confession of how she participated and aided the bandits in escape. While fighting back bitter tears, she made one request of the district attorney: to be tried anywhere but Pittsburgh, due to the courthouse being located across the street from her family's home. She, of course, claimed to want this for her family's sake and to spare her husband any more humiliation. Her husband, Peter Soffel, now ex-warden of the Allegheny County Penitentiary, retained counsel for her defense but made it clear that in the future he planned to have nothing to do with her. Soffel was not obliged her request of a change in venue and stood trial in Pittsburgh, was convicted and sentenced to two years in Western Penitentiary. She was released early for good behavior. After his wife's subsequent trial, the shamed Peter Soffel left Pittsburgh with his children and moved to Ohio, leaving his marriage and career behind. Peter eventually remarried. He and his children refused to make contact with his former wife even after she served her sentence.

In the aftermath of the escape, five jailers were discharged: Conrad Deitrich, the father of Mrs. Soffel; James McGeary because he carried the keys into the jail with him; George Kostow "because he showed bad judgment in the jail"; Charles Reynolds, the guard who was shot, because his story was contradictory to what actually transpired during the escape; and, lastly, Frank Chase because he knew of the affair between Soffel and Edward Biddle and failed to report it. This was discovered because Chase foolishly talked to friends and others outside of work, which ultimately got back to his superiors.

After her release, Mrs. Soffel attempted to take advantage of her plight and sell her scandalous story to the public by turning it into a play titled *They Died for Liberty*. This, sadly, did not yield the results she intended, and she abandoned her attempt at playwriting. With fame and fortune eluding

Form 144 (old 83). Prothonotary.

Allegheny County, ss.

The Commonwealth of Pennsylvania,

To *Kate Soffel nee Kate Dietrich* Greeting:

Whereas, *Peter K. Soffel*

did, on the *28th* day of *June* A. D.

190 *2*, present *his* petition to the Judges of

our Court of Common Pleas No. *3* of said County

of Allegheny, praying for the causes therein set forth

that *he* might be Divorced from the Bonds of Matrimony entered into with

you, the said *Kate Soffel nee Kate Dietrich*

We do therefore Command you, the said

Kate Soffel nee Kate Dietrich

that, setting aside all other business and excuses whatsoever, you be and appear,

in your proper person, before our said Judges, at the City of Pittsburgh, at a Court

of Common Pleas, No. *3* there to be holden for the County aforesaid, on the

first Monday of *August* next, to answer the Petition, or Libel, of

the said *Peter K. Soffel* and to show cause,

if any you have, why the said *Peter K. Soffel* your

husband should not be Divorced from the Bonds of Matrimony, agreeably to

the Acts of Assembly in such case made and provided. And hereof fail not.

Witness, the Honorable *John M. Kennedy* President

Judge of our said Court, at Pittsburgh, the *28th* day of *June* 190 *2*

Prothonotary.

A page from the divorce papers filed by Warden Peter Soffel in 1902. *Courtesy of the Library and Archives Division, Senator John Heinz Pittsburgh Regional History Center.*

her, she instead chose to become a seamstress, opening a shop on Maiden Lane on the North Side. Now the family pariah, alone and disgraced, Soffel abandoned her married name and chose instead to be called by her maiden name, Dietrich. She did not have to bear her shame too long, dying alone in 1909 from typhoid fever.

IN THE COURT OF COMMON PLEAS NO. 3 OF ALLEGHENY COUNTY.

Peter K. Soffel   (No. 399 August Term 1902.

     vs.   (In Divorce, a vinculo

Kate Soffel, nee   (matrimonii.

     Dietrich   (

To the Honorable the Judges of said Court, the petition of
Kate Soffel respectfully represents:

    That she is the respondent in the above entitled case
and has been served with a subpoena therein and has caused
an appearance to be entered for her by S. S. Robertson,
her attorney.

    That in the libel filed in the said case she is charged
with having been guilty of adultery with various men therein
named and other men whose names the libellant alleges are
unknown to him. That in particular she is charged with having
been guilty of adultery on the 31st day of January 1902, with
one Edward Biddle, now deceased.

    That she is not guilty of any of the offenses in the said
libel charged against her and has other matters of defense
which she is advised are sufficient in law to prevent a decree
for the libellant in the said case.

    That your petitioner is now confined in the Western
Penitentiary and by reason of such confinement can consult
with her attorney only with much difficulty and in consequence
of her said imprisonment is unable to assist her said attorney
in the procuring of witnesses to testify in her behalf. That
owing to the numerous charges made against her in the said
libel, if the libellant be permitted to proceed with his said

A page from a response filed by Kate Soffel during her divorce proceedings in 1902. It denied that she had committed adultery with Ed Biddle or any other inmate with whom she had contact in the Allegheny County Jail. *Courtesy of the Library and Archives Division, Senator John Heinz Pittsburgh Regional History Center.*

SELECTED BIBLIOGRAPHY

Archival Materials

Commonwealth v. Irene Schroeder alias Irene Schrader, March Term, 1930. Official Stenographic Record, 53rd Judicial District, New Castle, Pennsylvania.

Johnson, Paul G. "Glenn and Irene: The Life and Times of Glenn Dague and Irene Shrader Resulting in the Death of Corporal Brady Clemens Paul." 2005. MS 364.1523. New Castle Public Library.

Soffel Divorce Papers, 1996.0079. Library and Archives Division, Senator John Heinz Pittsburgh Regional History Center.

Articles

Atchinson Daily Globe. "Frank Cooley Dead." October 3, 1892.

Barcousky, Len. "Eyewitness 1818: No Jail Could Hold This Pittsburgh Thief." *Pittsburgh Post-Gazette*, March 22, 2009.

———. "Eyewitness 1927: Bethel Park Brinks Robbery Included Man Who'd Killed Cop." *Pittsburgh Post-Gazette*, October 30, 2011.

Barensfeld, Robert. "The Great Shoot-Out." *Milestones* 20, no. 3 (Fall 1995).

Bennett, Joe. "The Killer and the Warden's Wife." *Pittsburgh Press*, February 5, 1978.

Connellsville Courier. "The Cooley Court." December 9, 1892.

———. "The Cooley Gang Go Up." December 30, 1892.

———. "Frank Cooley Shot by a Farmer Lad, It Is Thought Seriously Wounded." September 30, 1892.

Daily National Intelligencer. "On Friday Last, J.F. Pluymart, One of the Persons Supposed to Have Been Concerned in the Robbery." June 16, 1818.

Donalson, Al. "Jail's Legendary Lovers' Escape May Become Film." *Pittsburgh Press*, June 19, 1983.

Emporia Daily Gazette. "Unarmed Clerk Overpowers Two Bank Robbers." September 20, 1941.

Evening Herald. "After the Cooley Gang." August 11, 1892.

———. "Bandit Cooley's End." October 3, 1892.

———. "Cooley Outlaws Attend Church." August 10, 1892.

———. "On the Trail of the Outlaws." July 8, 1892.

Evening Standard. "Pleads Guilty!" December 10, 1892.

———. "Prinkey's Denial." March 28, 1892.

———. "Ramsey Guilty!" December 9, 1892.

———. "Two Convicted!" December 7, 1892.

———. "A Wonderful Dreamer." March 3, 1892.

Genius of Liberty. "Bound and Gagged." June 14, 1888.

———. "Caught a Cooley." July 28, 1892.

———. "The Cooley Gang Rob Jacob Prinkey's House in Wharton Township." September 29, 1892.

———. "The Cooley's Are As Good As Done For." December 15, 1892.

———. "Frank Cooley Convicted and Awaiting Sentencing—Escapes from Jail." December 19. 1889.

———. "Frank Cooley Jailed and Released on Bail." December 27, 1888.

———. "Frank Cooley Killed." October 6, 1892.

———. "His Circle of Death." March 3, 1892.

———. "Indications That Ramsey Will Be Rammed into Prison Pretty Hard." December 13, 1892.

———. "Prinkey Pulled." March 3, 1892.

———. "Was It the Cooley Gang?" September 29, 1892.

———. "William Martin Family Tried for Larceny and Receiving Stolen Goods." December 8, 1892.

Greensburg Daily Tribune. "Fix Blame in Prison Break." May 4, 1933.

Huntingdon Daily News. "Judge Dismisses Hesitating Jury." October 5, 1933.

Indiana Evening Gazette. "Bank Robber Goes on Trial." December 10, 1941.

———. "Palmer Given Long Sentence." December 18, 1941.

———. "Road Agents at Work." May 25, 1908.

———. "Second Bank Robber Dies in Hospital." September 20, 1941.

Kodinsky, Harry. "Maug Baffles County Police, Ohio Deputy." *Pittsburgh Post-Gazette*, May 23, 1933.

McKeesport Daily News. "Englert's Story of the Shooting." June 6, 1908.

———. "Outlaws Put Up Fatal Battle." June 6, 1908.

———. "Thousands View Body of Robber." June 6, 1908.

The Milepost. "The Cooley Gang of Fairchance—Fayette Desperados." July 1995.

New Castle News. "Resume Search at Pittsburgh for Prisoners." May 18, 1933.

New York Times. "After a Gang of Outlaws." August 17, 1892.

———. "Autopsy on the Biddles." February 3,1902.

———. "Bandit Slayer of 7 Dies in Electric Chair." January 22, 1929.

———. "The Biddles and Mrs. Soffel." February 6, 1902.

———. "Biddles' Bodies on View." February 5, 1902.

———. "The Biddles Buried." February 6, 1902.

———. "The Biddles: To the Editor of the New York Times." February 9, 1902.

———. "Bound, Gagged and Robbed." July 14, 1891.

———. "Captive Tells of Hold-Up." July 14, 1929.

———. "Close to Train Bandits." July 3, 1911.

———. "Condemned Prisoners Break Out of Jail." January 31, 1902.

———. "The Cooleys Go to Church." August 9, 1892.

———. "Crime Thrill Told by Mrs. Schroeder." March 21, 1930.

———. "Dague Found Guilty, with Death Verdict." April 1, 1930.

———. "Don't Want to Die Together." November 19, 1901.

———. "Escaped Murderers Are Still at Liberty." August 20, 1927.

———. "Fight Murder Extradition." January 19, 1930.

———. "Five Jailers Discharged." April 9, 1902.

———. "45,000 on Train Bandits Held Up." July 2, 1911.

———. "Held as Train Bandits." July 7, 1911.

———. "Irene Goes to Place of Execution." February 22, 1931.

———. "Irene Schroeder Dies in the Chair." February 24, 1931.

———. "Jailbreakers Dead in Prison of Wounds." February 2, 1902.

———. "Jaworski Shooting Foils Escape Plot." September 15, 1928.

———. "Jaworski Trapped, Kills One Pursuer." September 14, 1928.

———. "Mrs. Kate Soffel Dead." August 30, 1909.

———. "Mrs. Schroeder Resigned." February 21, 1931.

———. "Mrs. Schroeder to Die at 7 This Morning." February 23, 1931.

———. "Mrs. Soffel Gets Two Years." May 11, 1902.

———. "Mrs. Soffel Indicted." March 14, 1902.

———. "Mrs. Soffel's Big Mail." February 9, 1902.

———. "Murder Plea Hearing Set." July 6, 1930.

———. "A Noted Robber Shot." December 29, 1891.

———. "Outlaw Cooley Shot Down." October 3, 1892.

———. "Pinchot Refuses Plea for Irene Schroeder." February 20, 1931.

———. "Pursuing Posse Shot Down Jail Breakers." February 1, 1902.

———. "Says Biddles Had Money." February 7, 1902.

———. "Seized in Canada As Pittsburgh Bandit." November 27, 1927.

———. "Six Pittsburgh Bandits Kill Advance Guard and Take $20,000 Christmas Payroll for Mine." December 24, 1922.

———. "Slain Man Brother of Schroeder Girl." January 8, 1933.

———. "Three Hold Up Bank; One Killed While Escaping." September 20, 1941.

———. "Three Men Shot in Train Hold-Up." July 1, 1911.

———. "Two Escaped Lifers Traced Here by Call." June 1, 1933.

———. "Will Try Jaworski Oct. 22." September 16, 1928.

———. "Woman Must Die for Killing Officer." August 10, 1930.

Paris, Barry. "True Story: Get the Goods on Mrs. Soffel." *Pittsburgh Post-Gazette*, February 23, 1985.

Patton, Carole. "Daring Escape Tries." *Pittsburgh Post-Gazette*, August 8, 1983.

Philadelphia Inquirer. "The Cooley Gang Again." September 22, 1891.

———. "The Cooley Gang Captured." August 20. 1892.

———. "The Cooley Gang's Crimes." June 24, 1891.

———. "Mrs. Soffel Stirs Interest in Case." February 24, 1985.

———. "A Peddler Attacked and Robbed." November 10, 1891.

Pittsburg Commercial Gazette. "Ramsey Trembled." December 10, 1892.

Pittsburg Dispatch. "After the Cooleys." November 19, 1891.

———. "After the Cooleys; A Fayette County Officer Hurrying to the Hiding Place of the Notorious Gang of Thieves." August 19, 1892.

———. "Another Cooley Crusade." July 28, 1892.

———. "Beats Jesse James." December 20, 1891.

———. "Betrayed by Frey." October 5, 1892.

———. "The Capture of the Cooleys." October 6, 1892.

———. "Cider and the Cooleys." February 25, 1892.

———. "A Circle of Death after the Cooleys." February 29, 1892.

———. "Compelled to Dig His Own Grave." March 12, 1892.

———. "Confesses to the Murder of Old Man Yost, Implicating Two Others." April 3, 1892.

———. "Cooley Boys' Nervy Act." August 4, 1891.

———. "The Cooley Brutes." September 10, 1892.

———. "The Cooley Cases." December 8, 1892.

———. "A Cooley Fake Punctured." December 29, 1891.

———. "A Cooley Haunt Raided." July 3, 1892.

———. "The Cooley Hunt." February 29, 1892.

———. "Cooley Laid to Rest." July 26, 1892.

———. "The Cooley Queen Caught." October 13, 1892.

———. "The Cooleys Again." July 27, 1892.

———. "Cooley's Audacious Gang." November 10, 1891.

———. "Cooley's Babe in the Penitentiary." December 30, 1892.

———. "Cooley's Gang Is Broken Up, Their Chief Dead, Jack Ramsey Captured, and No One Left to Lead Them." October 4, 1892.

———. "The Cooleys Gone." February 13, 1892.

———. "Cooleys Outwitted." July 29, 1892.

———. "The Cooleys Overruled." December 15, 1892.

———. "Cooley's Parents Nabbed." December 1, 1892.

———. "A Cooley Surprise." December 7, 1892.

———. "Cowed by the Cooleys." February 16, 1892.

———. "Dick Cooley's Dose." April 6, 1892.

———. "Frank Cooley Has a Double." September 15, 1892.

———. "Frank Cooley Now a Corpse." October 3, 1892.

———. "Frank Cooley Shot." September 27, 1892.

———. "Friends Saved Them." November 20, 1891.

———. "The Girls Jailed." October 7, 1892.

———. "Had Fun with Neighbors." April 2, 1892.

———. "He Got His Bedclothes." August 22, 1892.

———. "Jack Cooley Killed." July 24, 1892.

———. "Near the Rope's End." December 17, 1892.

———. "A New Campaign Against the Cooleys." February 21, 1892.

———. "Not a Dangerous Crowd." January 2, 1892.

———. "One of Fayette County's Masked Burglars Fails to Prove an Alibi." June 10, 1889.

———. "One of the Cooley Gang." February 23, 1892.

———. "One of the Cooley Gang Convicted." March 8, 1892.

———. "A Pesky Band Trying to Pose as Outlaws." August 7, 1892.

———. "A Petty Outlaw's Death." July 24 1892.

———. "The Protection of the Law." October 4, 1892.

———. "Ramsey Gives It Up." December 11, 1892.

———. "Six Cooley Fiends." August 3, 1892.

———. "The Slippery Cooleys." July 30, 1892.

———. "A Storm of Wrath." December 30, 1891.

———. "Tempered with Mercy." December 28, 1892.

———. "Terrorized by Bandits." June 24, 1891.

———. "There Is No Cooley Gang." December 31, 1891.

———. "Tracing the Cooleys." August 17, 1892.

———. "Train Robbers Foiled." June 14, 1892.

———. "Why the Cooleys Are at Large." November 20, 1891.

Pittsburgh Post-Gazette. "Criminal Interest: Jail Administrator Is a Lock for Person Who Knows Most about Biddle Brothers Breakout." June 13, 2001.

———. "Deputy Warden Marks Anniversary of Jail Break." January 30, 2002.

———. "Detective Ace Ordered Back to Beat." May 23, 1942.

———. "End of the Maug Mob." January 25, 1933.

———. "High Court Overrules Life Term." October 1, 1940.

———. "The Maug Escape." April 27, 1933.

———. "Maug Partner Robs Pair on Baldwin Road." May 9, 1933.

———. "Maug Reward Given to Four." June 30, 1933.

———. "Maug, Turpack Facing Quiz on Escape Today." June 19, 1933.

———. "Maug, Turpack to Return Today." June 17, 1933.

———. "Mob Killers Admit Murder of Constable." January 24, 1933.

———. "Noted Sleuth Is Victim of Heart Attack." April 27, 1935.

———. "Notorious Bandit of 1933 Winning Way to Freedom." May 14, 1952.

———. "Offer of $10,000 Spurs Maug Hunt." May 20, 1933.

———. "Plot of Prisoners to Saw Way Out of Pen Here Revealed." October 13, 1934.

———. "Two Accused of Helping in Maug Escape." May 10, 1933.

Pittsburgh Press. "Constable Slaying Listed As Unsolved." May 19, 1932.

———. "Gangster's Mother Weeps, Sweetheart Won't Talk." April 27, 1933.

———. "Gun Unidentified in Officers Death." October 31, 1932.

———. "Magnet Draws Two Guns from River." October 19, 1932.

———. "Maug and Turpack Flee Carrick Cop." May 5, 1933.

———. "Maug Escape Story Revealed." April 28, 1933.

———. "Maug Gang Bandit Asks Commutation." April 9, 1950.

———. "Maug Posse Raids Hill House in Vain." May 4, 1933.

———. "Maug Search on North Side Draws Blank." April 29, 1933.

———. "Maug Suspect Held for Court." May 7, 1933.

———. "Mob's Leader Is One of Four Fleeing Cells." April 27, 1933.

———. "Pistol Linked to Ross Killing." October 21, 1932.

———. "Police Fail to Find Hold-Up Men's Guns." October 10, 1932.

———. "Rich Payrolls Here Magnet to Bandits." December 7, 1930.

———. "Warden Suspects Two Guards in Maug Prison Break." May 1, 1933.

Preston County Journal. "Frank Cooley Dead." October 6, 1892.

———. "The Last of the Cooley Gang." October 27, 1892.

Reading Eagle. "Slayer in Cell; Blonde Mate Weds Soldier." June 17, 1933.

Sebak, Rick. "The Biddle Boys Stop for a Bite." *Pittsburgh Magazine*, February 2009.

———. "Gangster History in Bethel Park." *Pittsburgh Magazine*, July 23, 2009.

Sprigle, Ray. "Boss of the Flathead Killers." *Pittsburgh Post-Gazette*, April 3, 1949.

St. Paul Daily Globe. "End of the Cooley Cases." December 18, 1892.

Valley Star Monitor Herald. "Bandits Slain." September 21, 1941.

Wheeling Register. "The Bandit Buried." October 5, 1892.

———. "The Cooley Band of Outlaws." August 18, 1892.

———. "His Trousers Leg." July 17, 1892.

BOOKS

Atlas of Fayette County Pennsylvania. Philadelphia: G.M. Hopkins & Co., 1872.

Beal, Ronald L. *McKeesport Trolleys.* McKeesport, PA: Word Assn. Publisher, 1999.

Boucher, John Newton, and John W. Jordan. *A Century and a Half of Pittsburgh and Her People.* Vol. 2. New York: Lewis Publishing Company, 1908.

Burmester, Bill. "Crime and Violence." In *Legends of Lawrence County.* Marceline, MO: Walsworth, 1992.

Centennial Atlas of Allegheny County. Philadelphia: G.M. Hopkins & Co., 1876.

Forrest, Arthur. *The Biddle Boys and Mrs. Soffel.* Baltimore: Phoenix Publishing Company, 1902.

Mann, Henry. *Our Police: A History of the Pittsburgh Police Force Under the Town and City.* Pittsburgh: Henry Fenno, 1889.

Schalcosky, John D. *Ross Township (Images of America Series).* Charleston, SC: Arcadia Publishing Company, 2011.

Thurston, George. *Allegheny County's Hundred Years.* Pittsburgh: A.A. Anderson & Son, 1888.

Veitz, Dee Tabone. *Irene.* Punxsutawney, PA: Spirit Publishing, 1985.

Wilson, Erasmus, and Weston Arthur Goodspeed. *Standard History of Pittsburg Pennsylvania.* Chicago: H.R. Cornell & Co., 1898.

WEBSITES

Bosnyak, Stephen. "The Great Streetcar Robbery (1908)." www.dead-mans-hollow.com. Accessed March 25, 2012.

Hunt, Diana. "Ghost on Laurel Mountain (PA)." *Beanery Online Literary Magazine*, November 9, 2009. beanerywriters.wordpress.com/2009/11/09/ghost-on-laurel-mountain-pa. Accessed April 12, 2012.

Miller, Megan J. "Schroeder Case Made History." February 20, 2011. Accessed January 6, 2012. www.timesonline.com/news/ article_d678f464-3d6a-11e0-9514-00127992bc8b.html.

"Origins of the Allegheny County Police (Buck McGovern and the Biddle Boys)." www.county.allegheny.pa.us/police/origins.aspx. Accessed April 12, 2012.

"The Stories of Some Who Worked on the C&I." www.trainweb.org. Accessed March 5, 2012.

INDEX

A

Allebaugh, Joseph 35
Allegheny County 21, 22, 23, 25, 62,
    97, 101, 109
Allegheny County Jail 21, 22, 23, 60,
    64, 97, 101
Arizona 82
Arlington Hotel 74
armored car 17, 21

B

Baldwin, Eva 77
Barstad, George 23
Bassi, Mechleo 92
Beadling mine 19
Beaver River 54
Bellebridge Hill 94
Belsano 91
Bentleyville 18
Benwood 80
Bethel Park 17, 20
Biddle boys 95, 96, 97, 98, 99, 100,
    101, 102, 105, 106, 108, 109
Biddle, Ed 95, 97, 98, 99, 100, 101,
    103, 105, 106, 107, 109
Biddle, Jack 95, 100, 102, 105, 106, 107

Biggert, Roscoe 58, 60
Biggert, Wallace 58, 60
Blaney, Isaac 37
Block, C.H. 90
Bodziakowski, Stanley 21, 22
Bomford, Elmer 62
Book, George 77
Boston 93
Bowell, James 30
Braddock 18
Brenneman, Arthur 68
Bunker Hill Car Barns 58
Butler 18, 73, 74, 75, 84, 105, 106
Butler County 68, 104, 106
Byrnes, Thomas 58

C

Calvary Cemetery 109
Cambria and Indiana Railroad 91
Cambria County 91
Campbell, Frank 43
Carrick 62
Chase, Frank 109
Chestnut Ridge 29
Chloroform Gang 95, 97
Cincinnati 53, 74
circle of death 38, 39

Cleveland 23, 25, 62, 64, 65, 68
Collier, Thomas 41
Colonial Hotel 75, 77
Colver 91, 92
Cooley, Dick 29, 30, 38, 39
Cooley, Frank 29, 30, 31, 33, 34, 35,
    36, 37, 38, 39, 41, 42, 43, 44,
    45, 46, 47, 48, 49
Cooley Gang 28, 29, 30, 31, 33, 34,
    36, 37, 38, 39, 42, 43, 44, 45,
    46, 47, 49
Cooley, Jack 29, 34, 36, 37, 38, 40, 41,
    48
Cooley, Lute 29, 33, 41, 46, 49
Cooley, Oliver 30
Cooley, William 30
Coverdale mine 17
Crawford, Tom 74, 76, 77, 78
Crowley, Martin J. 75
Crowl, Mollie 77, 78
Cummings, Matt 91

D

Dague, Glenn 73, 74, 76, 77, 78, 79,
    80, 81, 82, 83, 84, 88
David, Charlie 30, 49
Davis, Joseph 91
DeCarlo, Angelo 70
Deitrich, Conrad 109
Delany's Cave 31
Detroit 17, 18, 19, 20, 22, 23, 67
Dorman, Walter 96, 97
Dowling, Irene 62
dynamite 60, 65, 91

E

Ebensburg Coal Company 91
Effinger, George 23
electric chair 21, 25, 73, 88, 92
Elizabeth 93
Ellwood City 69, 70
Emmons, Herman 51, 52, 53, 54

Englert, John 94
Erie 62, 89, 90, 91
Evarts, Virgil 67, 68, 69, 70
Ewing, Charles 34

F

Fairchance 27, 29, 31, 34, 38, 41, 42,
    43, 44, 46, 47
Fairchance Furnace Company 36
Farmers' and Mechanics' Bank 51,
    54, 56
Farrell 68
Fayette County 27, 29, 31, 33, 34, 35,
    36, 37, 39, 43, 44, 46, 47, 48,
    49, 67
Feelo, Albert 67, 68, 69, 70
Fine, George 65
Fisher, George 46, 47
Fitzgerald, Patrick 96
Flaherty, John 58
Flathead Gang 17, 18, 19, 20, 21, 22,
    23, 64
Flory, Daniel 58
Foster, William 34
Franklin Township 34
Fried, Charles 91
Friedel, Edna 58, 61
Fried, Henry 91
Frye, Brent 30

G

Gaffney, William 64
Garman, James 91, 92
Geisler, Theodore Joseph 60
Georges Township 36, 41
Georges Township School Board 39,
    43
Gibbon's Glade 45
Graske, Edward 64
Greene County 38
Greensburg 74
Gump, Isaiah 20, 21

H

Harrington, Thomas 91
Harrisville Bank 68
Hartman, Ernest 69, 70, 71
Haydentown 34, 38
Hildebrand, Carl 58
Hill District 62
Hughes, Rex 68
Humbert, Samuel 27, 28, 29, 31
Hutchinson, Jim 30

I

Ingram Car Barn 58

J

Jackson, Gladys 58, 60, 64
Jaworski, Paul 17, 18, 19, 20, 21, 23, 25, 64
Jaworski, Sam 21, 22, 23

K

Kahney, Thomas 95
Kash, Laura 70
Keating Car Barns 57
Kiessling, William 82
King, Frank 91
Kingwood 44
Koudela, Yaro 25
Krenicky, Stephen "Mooch" 65

L

Lal, William 57
Lawrence County 67, 83
Layton Station 39
Lecky, William 53
Lewis, Charles 30
Lewis Gang 30, 31
Longanecker, W.A. 44

M

Majstrek, Benjamin 23
Manning, Thomas 94
Martin, James 91
Martin, William 30, 49
Mashey, George 37
Masontown 44
Maug Gang 57, 58, 59
Maug, John 57, 58, 59, 60, 61, 62, 64, 65
McClellandtown 29, 30
McCormick, George 34, 38, 40, 41, 42, 43, 46
McCormick, James 36
McCormick, Milt 47
McCullough, Mintie 30
McGeary, James 100, 109
McGovern, Charles "Buck" 95, 96, 104, 105, 106
McKeesport 93
McKeesport Hospital 94
Mentch, Warren 91, 92
Mercer County 68
Meyers, George 37
Meyers, Rufus 37, 39
Mifflin Township 62
Miller, Beryl 80
Missouri 74
Mollenauer mine 20
Monaca 80
Monongahela River 52, 59
Monongalia County 37
Moore, Earnest 75, 77, 78, 83, 88
Moran, Joseph 91
Morgan, Daniel 51, 54
Morgan, Frank 59
Morgan, Thomas 59
Moses, Vernon Porter 57, 58, 59
Moulden, Herman 58, 60
Mount Chestnut 105
Mount Washington 97
Mowry, John 93
Moyer, Charles 57, 59

N

Neville, Morgan 51
New Castle 68, 73, 75, 77, 78, 80, 81, 83, 88
New York 54

O

Ohio 18, 20, 53, 60, 62, 74, 79, 80, 109
Ohio River 53, 54

P

Palmer, Kenneth 67, 68, 69, 70
Paluszynski, Paul. *See* Jaworski, Paul
Parkersburg 80
Pasta, James 69, 70, 71
Pastorious, Lyda 30, 33, 38, 39, 42, 44, 49
Patterson, John 94
Paul, Brady 75, 77, 78, 84, 88
Pegg, Frank 46, 47
Perrysville 102
Perrysville Avenue 102
Pezzi, Anthony 92
Piccus, Norman 64
Pittsburg Dispatch 34, 36, 44
Pittsburgh 17, 18, 19, 20, 22, 23, 34, 36, 39, 51, 53, 54, 55, 56, 57, 59, 61, 62, 65, 74, 95, 97, 101, 102, 105, 106, 107, 109
Pittsburgh Motor Coach Company 58
Pittsburgh Post-Gazette 64
Pittsburgh Terminal Coal Company 17
Pluymart, Joseph 51, 52, 53, 54, 55
Point Breeze 62
Potts, Delmar 64
Prescott, Rueben 93
Preston County 36, 37, 38, 39
Prince, Freddie 60
Prinkey, Jacob 45, 46, 48
Prohibition 58
Prospect 105

R

Ramsey, Jack 29, 31, 35, 38, 39, 40, 41, 45, 46, 47, 48
Rankin, Ed 43
Reed, Jesse 93
Reserve Township 58
Reynolds, Charles 109
Rhodes, John 30
Robinson, Bill 38
Rockview Penitentiary 25, 67, 88
Rohrer's Gun Store 68
Rooney, H.D. 89, 90
Rosenstein, Joel 35
Ross, Mollie 31, 33
Ross Township 57, 102
Ryan, Frank 91

S

Schroeder, Donnie 74, 78, 80, 81, 83, 88
Schroeder, Irene 73, 74, 76, 77, 78, 79, 80, 81, 82, 83, 84, 88
Schulze, John Andrew 56
Shaffer, Edward 69, 70, 71
Shenango Township 75
Sisler, Wesley 39, 42
Smithfield 34, 38, 41, 44, 48, 67
Smith, William 44
Soffel, Katherine 97, 98, 99, 100, 101, 104, 105, 107, 109
Soffel, Peter 97, 109
Sprigle, Ray 19, 25
Stemmler, Alexander 58
Stemmler, Eleanor 58
St. Louis 81
Sutton, Daniel 38

T

Tennessee 74
Toledo 74
Turner, William 30, 37, 39
Turpack, Edward 57, 59, 60, 61, 62, 64, 65

U

Ukraine 18
Uniontown 29, 33, 37, 38, 39, 43, 45, 46, 67, 74

V

Vasabinder, Jack 21
Volant 67

W

Walters, John 44
Washington County 18, 21
Weckoski, Joseph 18
Weller, Christopher R. 103
Wells, Joe 82
Western Penitentiary 56, 60, 61, 64, 109
Western Union 62, 64
Westmoreland County 44
West View 102
West Virginia 36, 37, 39, 44, 48, 53, 73, 79, 80
Wharton Township 45
Wheeling 53, 73, 79, 80
White House Inn 103
Wieczorek, Anthony 23, 25
Wiley's Livery 93
Woods, Tom 43
Wynn Coke Works 43

Y

Yeager, Sam 30, 37, 38, 39, 46, 49
Youngstown 18

Z

Zygello, Chester 58

ABOUT THE AUTHORS

Thomas White is the university archivist and curator of special collections in the Gumberg Library at Duquesne University. He is also an adjunct lecturer in Duquesne's History Department and an adjunct professor of history at La Roche College. White received a master's degree in public history from Duquesne University. Besides the folklore and history of Pennsylvania, his areas of interest include public history and American cultural history. He is the author of *Legends and Lore of Western Pennsylvania*, *Forgotten Tales of Pennsylvania*, *Ghosts of Southwestern Pennsylvania*, *Forgotten Tales of Pittsburgh* and *Forgotten Tales of Philadelphia* (coauthored with Edward White), all published by The History Press.

Michael Hassett is a recent graduate of La Roche College, where he earned a bachelor's degree in history and political science. It is at La Roche where he met and studied under Thomas White, assisting with editing and research for his previous books. Michael is currently an Americorps volunteer, where he works with and mentors Pittsburgh's inner-city youth. He is also a Peace Corps nominee and hopes to be placed in the fall of 2012 for service. His areas of interest include colonial and modern U.S. history and American folklore.

Visit us at
www.historypress.net

www.ingramcontent.com/pod-product-compliance
Lightning Source LLC
Chambersburg PA
CBHW060809100426
42813CB00004B/998